T0348786

Scholarly Communication in China, Hong Kong, Japan, Korea and Taiwan

CHANDOS
PUBLISHING SERIES

Chandos' new series of books are aimed at all those individuals interested in publishing. They have been specially commissioned to provide the reader with an authoritative view of current thinking. If you would like a full listing of current and forthcoming titles, please visit our website, **www.chandospublishing.com**, or contact Hannah Grace-Williams on e-mail info@chandospublishing.com or telephone number +44 (0) 1993 848726.

New authors: we are always pleased to receive ideas for new titles. If you would like to write a book for Chandos, please contact Dr Glyn Jones on e-mail gjones@chandospublishing.com or telephone number +44 (0) 1993 848726.

Bulk orders: some organisations buy a number of copies of our books. If you are interested in doing this, we would be pleased to discuss a discount. Please contact Hannah Grace-Williams on e-mail info@chandospublishing.com or telephone number +44 (0) 1993 848726.

Scholarly Communication in China, Hong Kong, Japan, Korea and Taiwan

EDITED
BY
JINGFENG XIA

Chandos Publishing
Oxford · England

Chandos Publishing (Oxford) Limited
TBAC Business Centre
Avenue 4
Station Lane
Witney
Oxford OX28 4BN
UK
Tel: +44 (0) 1993 848726 Fax: +44 (0) 1865 884448
Email: info@chandospublishing.com
www.chandospublishing.com

First published in Great Britain in 2008

ISBN:
978 1 84334 322 6 (hardback)
1 84334 322 3 (hardback)

© The contributors, 2008

British Library Cataloguing-in-Publication Data.
A catalogue record for this book is available from the British Library.

Contents

About the editor

Jingfeng Xia is assistant professor in the School of Library and Information Science at Indiana University, Indianapolis. He received his master's degree in information resources and library science from the University of Arizona, where he also gained a PhD in anthropology. As an undergraduate he studied history at Peking University, China. He worked as a curator in different museums in China and the USA; then in the past few years his career has switched from anthropology to information resources and library science. In addition to experience as an information technology professional in the private sector, he has worked with digital libraries at the University of Arizona (School of Information Resources and Library Science) and the University of Florida's Smathers Libraries. He has also worked as a reference and instructional librarian in social sciences at Rutgers University Libraries.

His research interests focus on scholarly communication and digital repositories and libraries. With practice in digital repositories and metadata management, he has concentrated his studies on information identification and evaluation. He has consistently contributed to this research and will continue working on it. His research also includes exploring the applications of geographic information systems (GIS) in library and information management. Particularly, he has been applying GIS technologies to assist the management of library spaces and collection development. He has published many peer-reviewed articles in the above-mentioned areas.

Jingfeng Xia may be contacted at: *xiaji@iupui.edu.*

About the contributors

Hitoshi Kamada is associate librarian for Japanese studies at the University of Arizona. He completed his master's in library and information science at the University of Western Ontario, and also gained a master's in public administration at the University of Victoria and a BA in history at Doshisha University in Kyoto, Japan. His previous publications and presentations include studies on publishing and scholarly communication in Japan, such as 'Kiyo and scholarly communication in Japan', *Portal: Libraries and the Academy*, 7(3), July 2007; 'Incorporating a Japanese material approval plan in a changing collection development environment at the University of Arizona', *Collection Management*, 29(1): 3–17, September 2004; and 'East Asian collections and organizational transformation in academic libraries', *College & Research Libraries*, 63(2): 125–37, March 2002.

Joy Kim is the curator of the Korean Heritage Library at the University of Southern California. She has a BA in library science from Ewha Woman's University in Seoul, Korea, and a MLS degree from the University of California, Los Angeles. She worked as Japanese cataloger at the Los Angeles Public Library before moving to her current position. A recognized authority on Korean librarianship outside Korea, she consulted for major American universities on developing new Korean studies collections. She is the editor of *Korean Librarianship Outside of Korea: A Practical Guide and Manual* (Seoul: Asian Culture Press for the Committee on Korean Materials, Council on East Asian Libraries, Association for Asian Studies, 2002), and compiler of the *Library of Congress Subject Headings Related to Korea and General East Asia* ([Sl] Committee on East Asian Libraries, Association for Asian Studies, 1989). She has also published several articles in the USA and Korea on Korean studies librarianship in the USA.

Eun-Kyung Kwon is professor of library and information science at Daegu University, where she is also the director of the University Library. She has a BA and a PhD in library and information science from

Ewha Woman's University in Seoul, Korea, and an MEd from the University of Tokyo in Japan. She has published many articles on librarianship, including two on scholarly communication. She is a co-author of two books: *Collection Management* (Seoul: Kumi Trading, 1995 – in Korean; title translated), and *Collection Management in the Digital Age* (Seoul: Korean Library Association, 2005 – in Korean; title translated). Her major research interest is school libraries. Her current research involves school libraries/media centers in Korea.

Steven K. Luk received his PhD from Harvard University and his bachelor degree from the Chinese University of Hong Kong. He is currently the managing director and general manager of the Commercial Press (HK), and has been a part-time teacher of modern Japanese history and US-East Asian relations since January 2002. Dr Luk is the chairman of the Hong Kong Publishing Professional Society (since 1999), a council member of the Hong Kong Publishing Federation (since its establishment in 1996), fellow and executive committee member of the Institute of Print-media Professionals, honorary secretary of the Asian Studies Association of Hong Kong (since 2005), a deputy chairman of the editorial board of *The Journal of Hong Kong Society of Accountants* (2001–2003), chairman/member of the departmental advisory boards for both Lingnan University and Baptist University in Hong Kong and the Chinese University of Hong Kong and an adviser/appraiser at the Hong Kong Arts Development Council for literacy art. He is a well-known academic publisher in Asia, having jointly published the electronic version of the *Sikuquanshu* (*The Library of Four Chambers of Literature*) in 2000 and initiated *The China Review: An Interdisciplinary Scholarly Journal on Modern China* in 2002. He is often interviewed by the media on books and publishing as well as the trends of book reading in Hong Kong.

Mei-Mei Wu is professor of the Graduate Institute of Library & Information Studies at National Taiwan Normal University, Taipei, Taiwan, ROC. She received her MLIS and PhD in the School of Communication, Information and Library Studies at Rutgers University. Her doctoral dissertation was entitled *Information Interaction Dialogue: A Study of Patron Elicitation in the Information Retrieval Interaction*. Her research interests are information literacy, information behavior, scholarly communication, digital learning object repositories and e-learning. Her research projects include building and evaluation of digital learning object repositories, instructional design in the online teaching environment, training online tutors and facilitators, teachers' personal knowledge management, Chinese information retrieval systems evaluation and information resources for self-paced learners. She teaches collection development, scholarly communication, information psychology and research methods. Her research publications appear in both Chinese and English, in monographs, the *Journal of the American Society for Information Science and Technology* and *Information Processing & Management*, and include book chapters and conference papers.

Acknowledgements

In writing this book, we drew heavily on the past and current literature, various websites and other resources, for which we are deeply grateful. Because of space limitations, we cannot list each individual resource. We want particularly to thank Keith Trimmer and Kenneth Klein, librarians at the University of Southern California, for their editorial help in the writing of the Korea chapter; and David Xia for his comments on the draft of the China chapter. The editor is grateful to Lynn Mullins and Rowland Bennett, who provided assistance during the preparation of the book proposal. Most importantly, the editor wishes to express his gratitude to Dr Glyn Jones of Chandos Publishing (Oxford) for his invitation to work on a book on such an interesting subject, and his assistance during the planning and preparation of the manuscript. Cherry Ekins of Chandos Publishing (Oxford) worked hard on polishing the book drafts, which is appreciated.

List of acronyms

AAUP	Association of American University Presses
ACRL	Association of College & Research Libraries
A&HCI	Arts and Humanities Citation Index
AMS	American Mathematical Society
ARL	Association of Research Libraries
BIBF	Beijing International Book Fair
CADAL	China-American Digital Academic Library
CALIS	Chinese Academic Libraries & Information System
CAS	Chinese Academy of Sciences
CASS	Chinese Academy of Social Sciences
CC	Creative Commons
CIP	Cataloging in Print
COE	Center of Excellence
CONCERT	Consortium on Core Electronic Resources in Taiwan
CONWIS	Consortium of Wiley International Serials
CSCC	Committee on Scholarly Communication with China
DDS	document delivery service
DPRK	Democratic People's Republic of Korea
EI	Engineering Index
ELNP	National Science & Technology for e-Learning Program (Taiwan)
ELT	English language teaching
FOSS	Free and Open Source Software
GDP	gross domestic product
GERD	gross expenditure on R&D
GIS	geographical information systems
HKIED	Hong Kong Institute of Education
ICT	information and communications technology
IFLA	International Federation of Library Associations and Institutions

ILL	interlibrary loan
IMF	International Monetary Fund
ISBN	International Standard Book Number
ISRC	International Standard Recording Code
ISSN	International Standard Serial Number
JANUL	Japan Association of National University Libraries
KAOAS	Korea Association of Academic Societies
KCI	Korean Citation Index
KERIS	Korean Education and Research Information Service
KESLI	Korean Electronic Site License Initiative
KISS	Korean Studies Information Service System
KISTI	Korea Institute of Science and Technology Information
KISTI-ACOMS	KISTI Article Contribution Management System
KOMARC	Korean Machine Readable Catalog
KORSA	Korea Resource Sharing Alliance
KOSEF	Korea Science and Engineering Foundation
KRF	Korea Research Foundation
KRTRC	Korean Reprographic and Transmission Rights Center
KSI	Korean Studies Information
METS	Metadata Encoding and Transmission Standards
NACSIS	National Center for Science Information Systems (Japan)
NALK	National Assembly Library of Korea
NARL	National Applied Research Laboratories (Taiwan)
NCC	North American Coordinating Council on Japanese Library Resources
NCL	National Central Library (Taiwan)
NDAP	National Digital Archives Program (Taiwan)
NDSL	National Digital Science Library (Korea)
NESLI	National Electronic Site Licence Initiative (UK)
NII	National Institute of Informatics (Japan)
NLC	National Library of China
NLK	National Library of Korea
NSC	National Science Council (Taiwan)
NSFC	National Natural Science Foundation of China
OCLC	Online Computer Library Center
OECD	Organization for Economic Cooperation and Development

OSSF	Open Source Software Foundry
OUP	Oxford University Press
PLA	People's Liberation Army
PPP	purchasing power parity
R&D	research and development
RISS	Research Information Service System (Korea)
RLG	Research Library Group (USA)
ROC	Republic of China
ROK	Republic of Korea
SAR	Special Administrative Region
SCI	Science Citation Index
SCIE	Science Citation Index Expanded
SPARC	Scholarly Publishing and Academic Resources Coalition
SSCI	Social Science Citation Index
STM	sciences, technology and medicine
TAIR	Taiwan Academic Institutional Repository
TANet	Taiwan Academic Network
TEBNET	Taiwan EBook Net
TIBE	Taipei International Book Exhibition
TRS	Toshokan Ryūtsū Sentā
TRIPS	Agreement on Trade Related Aspects of Intellectual Property Rights
TSSCI	Taiwan Social Science Citation Index
UCC	Universal Copyright Convention
UNESCO	UN Economic, Social and Cultural Organization
WTO	World Trade Organization

Preface

Julia Gelfand

Inspiration for this volume was perhaps born in a course I taught at the University of Arizona on information and communications technology and global librarianship; the editor was enrolled in this course, and completed a marvelous and insightful paper, 'Scholarly communication in East and Southeast Asia: traditions and challenges'. That paper was revised, expanded and subsequently published, and served as the impetus to examine more seriously the issues of scholarly communication in the entire area (Xia, 2006). This edited volume explores important issues relevant to scholarly communication and how it has evolved, with chapters written by colleagues who are experts in its specific details and practices and who are familiar with this large and diverse area.

The definition of scholarly communication has only been in our standard lexicon since 1992, when Anthony Cummings and colleagues edited the report of probably the first project on these themes, funded by the Andrew W. Mellon Foundation, *University Libraries and Scholarly Communications* (Cummings et al., 1992). The library and publishing communities were well aware of individual elements that contributed to the crisis in scholarly publishing and communication, and found them increasingly important and interrelated, requiring greater attention by all stakeholders, including authors, editors, translators, publishers, information providers, libraries, distributors and vendors, and users, readers and scholars.

The Association of Research Libraries (ARL) and the American Association of Universities almost immediately joined forces to address and study the problems identified in the Cummings report, and concentrated on three major themes: foreign acquisitions, scientific and technological information and intellectual property. The ARL has served as a prominent leader in these efforts, creating a division focused on the topic, holding meetings with attendees coming from around the world, serving as an information clearing-house and establishing initiatives for its members to consider, participate in and adopt at their institutions. These issues included the economics of scholarly publishing, digital and distance learning and scholarship, and the range of outputs associated with these and related themes. Countries around the world followed suit and established their own way of addressing these global concerns.

The Association of College & Research Libraries Division of the American Library Association thereafter created a scholarly communication toolkit to assist the academic library community to work with faculty to understand the key issues better, and develop strategies for change that could introduce methods and best practices in scholarly communication and how it can be approached in different environments. The definition of scholarly communication for those purposes is:

> Scholarly communication is the system through which research and other scholarly writings are created, evaluated for quality, disseminated to the scholarly community, and preserved for future use. One of the fundamental characteristics of scholarly research is that it is created to facilitate inquiry and knowledge. The majority of scholars develops and disseminates their research with little or no expectation of direct financial reward. (Association of College & Research Libraries, 2006)

The history of scholarly conduct, printing and libraries in Asia has early beginnings in China, Japan and Korea. Without trying to respond to all the issues, but instead focusing on higher education and scholarly pursuits, a few developments stand out and deserve recognition. Since 1979 the Committee on Scholarly Communication with China (CSCC) in conjunction with the National Academy of Sciences, the Social Sciences Research Council and the American Council for Learned Societies has administered and sponsored research on China and promoted scholarly collaboration between Chinese and academic communities around the world. With the opening of the CSCC Beijing office in 1985, even more opportunities for exchange and collaboration were possible among scholars, and their need to disseminate their research findings worldwide prompted new models of publishing and distribution in many disciplines. This evolution in China and accelerated knowledge generation throughout Asia became a competitive and enterprising experience.

Additional information was compiled by many people around the globe as higher education and scholarly communication issues in Asia became more visible to the rest of the world. Several recent books have attempted to cover aspects of the content addressed in this volume. The topic is usually covered in books with a wider scope about global librarianship, only including scholarly communication as a slim chapter. International conferences have also been held to discuss scholarly communication in Asia, one of which was the e-workshop on Scholarly Communication in the Digital Era conducted at Feng Chia University, Taichung, Taiwan, in August 2003. Early proponents of education about scholarly communication from the USA and Canada assembled at that workshop, and leaders in higher education, publishing and academic libraries from Asia began serious study about the situation in their region.

Fast forward to the work of this volume, which combines an overview of scholarly communication in China, Hong Kong, Japan, Korea, Macao and Taiwan with both a landscape of the region and far more specificity and currency on issues of scholarly communication.

Each chapter offers a historical background, followed by insights and trends in academic infrastructures in these countries and regions, the role of government and how the evolution of electronic publishing and scholarship demonstrates both the ubiquity of these transformations over time and the unique attributes that characterize each country and region. Most interesting is the inclusion and treatment of the new and changing roles of national, academic and specialized libraries, growing emphasis on research and development and a rise in cooperative and collaborative partnerships between governments, professional societies and the private sector. This leads to an increase in scholarly output in both academic circles and commercial processes. Reading trends, although stable, are increasingly influenced by the global marketplace, the number of volumes available in translation and the movement to distribute works created in Asia more universally by establishing better distribution channels that promote them via the internet and other means.

Changes in electronic publishing products have accelerated due to the World Wide Web. Short and concentrated experiences with CD-ROMs in the early days of electronic publishing and scholarship made content very shareable and searchable, but neither intuitive nor user- and institution-friendly if not employed in a networked environment. With connectivity and access sometimes still problematic, but always increasing, and the internet flourishing, we experience new challenges. The preferred and perfected method of communicating, researching and increasingly reading via the web makes access a key component as more scholarly products are found in digital libraries and distance education becomes more prolific on an international scale.

Readers will gain an immense overview about the current situation of scholarly communication in Asia, and can easily conclude that enormous strides have been made in little more than a decade due to the prevalence of the internet and refinements in communication methods. Apologies are made by contributors for the incompleteness of this picture. Far less is known about North Korea, and keeping up with the rapid changes suggests that there may be omissions. However, this book provides a critical examination of scholarly communication in these countries and regions, traces how it has developed and introduces the reader to all the contributing players. Today, academic exchange in Asia is hugely popular, travel is widespread even to remote locations, the internet allows for greater connectivity and communication and scholarly outputs are prolific. The electronics industries in all these countries are robust and growing, librarianship as a profession is thriving, and together this offers additional solutions to new problems in the scholarly communication arena. Globalization truly accounts for much of this, but the increasing details create a need to organize and share information. How to be mindful of legal issues and finally generate new knowledge is critical to a better understanding of scholarly communication. The process is cyclical and contributes to some ambiguity, while encouraging an entrepreneurial spirit. New advances will continue to be made with partners from all parts of the world. 'Create Change',[1] the name of one of the ARL initiatives, still accurately informs each of these chapters and makes for a most educational and enjoyable reading experience. The title of the book aptly describes the contents and provides insights into how scholarly communication is perceived and treated in China, Hong Kong, Japan, Korea, Macao and Taiwan in very meaningful ways.

Julia Gelfand
University of California, Irvine
July 2007

Note

1. The Scholarly Publishing and Academic Resources Coalition (SPARC), the Association of Research Libraries (ARL) and the Association of College & Research Libraries (ACRL) in 2001 introduced the concept of 'Create Change' as a comprehensive advocacy resource with both print and online

components. Librarians and campus administrators have used the Create Change brochure to raise scholarly awareness of the impact that fast-rising journal prices have on scholarly communication. The brochure, which was updated in 2004, can be distributed in campus mailings and used in presentations to university departments and at educational programs on scholarly communication – see www.arl.org/sparc/media/2004-0106.html.

Introduction

Jingfeng Xia

Scholarly communication is the process of creating, evaluating, disseminating and preserving research and other scholarly writings. This process cannot be fully understood without a discussion of the higher education that delivers and advances knowledge and research methodology, the publishing industry that evaluates and disseminates intellectual ideas, the academic community, such as professional associations and foundations, that regulates and promotes scholarly activities, and the libraries that preserve and circulate scholarly materials. Recently, the rapid development of information and communications technology has metamorphosed the landscape of scholarly activities and redesigned the modules of information dissemination and preservation. Unprecedented opportunities to advance the conduct of scholarship have been created by the networked digital environment. These become the topics of concentration in this book. At the same time, some other issues related to scholarly conduct, such as copyright and censorship, are also included.

Each chapter introduces the practice of scholarly communication in one geographic region or country of East Asia. Each pays attention to its history and current condition by presenting both challenges and achievements that the region or country has experienced in the past and present, upon which upcoming trends in scholarly communication are projected. Moreover, the narrative describes how globalization has become part of intellectual pursuits on this side of the world, and how native traditions remain woven through the tapestry of daily scholarly practices.

Scholarly communication in China

Jingfeng Xia

Scholarly communication is better understood if discussed in the historical context of a country. The creation, transformation and exchange of intellectual ideas at any given time period echo concurrent economic developments, political exercises, technological innovations and cultural norms, creating a unique system that connects the past and future. With such a historical perspective, this chapter sketches the practice of scholarly communication throughout history in mainland China, with a concentration on modern society. A chronological description is organized so that readers can observe the trajectory of development in scholarly activities.

Classical legacy (prior to the late nineteenth century)

As one of the oldest, continuous civilizations in the world, China has a history of some 5,000 years, tracing back to the Three Sovereigns and Five Emperors. The earliest form of systematic writing was dated to the sixteenth century BC, when oracle bones were carved with symbols for divination in the Shang dynasty. These became the oldest historical documents with written symbols. The scripts were invented to decipher the messages sent to humans about the future by mysterious powers. Successive written languages included bronze inscriptions and scripts etched on to bamboo and wooden strips, the latter being the early forms of the so-called 'classical Chinese', the language that was used, though with modified styles over time, for more than 2,000 years until the late nineteenth and early twentieth centuries. The writings on bamboo, wood and, later, clothing existed for several centuries, during which scholars, including the famous philosopher Confucius, carried rolls of the strips to record and propagate their intellectual ideas.

One of the most influential contributions that the Chinese made to the development of scholarly communication was paper. This invention is credited to Cai Lun (circa 105 AD), who made improvements to earlier techniques using bark and hemp. The technology soon gained popularity and expedited the growth of modern books and monographs. Centuries later, paper gradually spread to the rest of the world along the Silk Road and other routes.

Another major contribution is the invention of printing, which experienced improvements from woodblock printing to movable type. The former was the technique of carving out a page of characters on to a wooden block, which was used to copy the text into a book, while the latter constructed pieces, rather than blocks, of moistened clay to form individually carved characters. Pieces of movable type could then be assembled to reflect the text of the book being printed. Such technological novelties have since then changed the fundamentals of scholarly communication and have extended well into modern printing all over the world.

Recorded scholarly activities can be found as early as the appearance of writing, starting with the exploration of religion, philosophy, literature and history. In the early years from 770 to 221 BC, history witnessed a flourishing of philosophical contention, known as the Hundred Schools of Thought. It was a period of vast cultural and intellectual expansion, characterized by itinerant scholars who debated ideologies and advised state leaders on matters of government and warfare. Famous philosophical schools emerged, including Confucianism, Taoism, legalism, Mohism, yin and yang and eclectics, competing with and supplementing each other, profoundly influencing social consciousness even in present-day East Asia. This richness of scholarly debate mirrored a changing political world where wars among state and regional powers were intensifying and class struggles escalated.

With the introduction and later sophistication of numerous different philosophies during this period, many classic writings were created that became the basis of Chinese practices in virtually every aspect of life for the next two-and-a-half millennia. These philosophers were famous teachers who passed their ideas to students and followers through lectures, discussions and publications. Confucius alone had more than 3,000 disciples. These philosophers were also book collectors who pioneered private libraries in Chinese history.

The decades-long chaos of combat and rational discord of the Hundred Schools of Thought was ended by Qin Shi Huang, who conquered and unified different states to form China in 221 BC. Self-proclaimed as the first emperor, he set up a system of centralized autocratic power that endured for over 2,000 years. His reforms fundamentally changed every aspect of society, both at his time and afterwards. Among other reforms, the standardization of writing, law, scholarship, bureaucracy and weights and measures expedited the formation of the Chinese convention of scholarly communication, characterized by homogeneity resulting from tight control. As a step to accomplish this standardization, the emperor decreed that scholars of the non-legalism school should be buried alive, virtually all the books from previous regimes not written by imperial historians should be burnt, free scholarly discussions were banned and only books he liked were allowed.

Successive dynasties extended the reformed system with minor adjustments necessary to their situations, e.g. Confucianism was revived to replace legalism as the official ideology of many imperial states. For a long time scholarly activities were carried out under suffocating censorship that encouraged a strong concentration on the humanities. Although the developments of science and technology had produced many amazing discoveries, such as the inventions of the compass and gunpowder and achievements in mathematical investigations, astronomical observations and medical advances, literature, history and philosophy were commonly recognized as the core of scholarly pursuits.

Such a literature, history and philosophy orientation was strengthened by the formulation of an imperial examination system, *ke ju*, in about 606 AD. This national public examination was designed to select capable government officials from intellectuals by a test of essay writing on the topics of literature, history and government strategies. The essay styles gradually developed and imitated a common model, *ba gu wen*, known for its rigid form and lack of ideas, which unfortunately discouraged creativity. When *ke ju* became the major way to achieve wealth and high status, schooling was designed to target the examinations and learning changed its intrinsic values from idealism to utilitarianism.

The perceptions of learning and teaching are deeply rooted in particular cultural antecedents and social values. From its beginning, the educational concept had been inspired by Confucian principles which emphasized the high importance placed on education by society and encouraged the integration of learning and thinking. Learning was not only important for cultivating oneself as an intellectual person, but was also a moral obligation for the good of family and society.

With *ke ju* being an unfortunate addition to the educational system, the style, content and structure of the examination redirected the teaching-learning philosophy. A learning process that necessitated rote memorization and required students to be passive receivers discouraged independent thinking. Students were viewed as sponges of authoritative knowledge, while teachers were responsible for transmitting that knowledge by strictly following specially designed handbooks. Both official and private schools (e.g. *si shu*, a popular form of education where either students learned at a teacher's home or a wealthy family hired a teacher to provide on-site tuition to the family's children) urged students to accept and conform to the established principles and procedures, and advised them to memorize in order to get good grades. Under this system, students were more comfortable with accumulating knowledge systematically than proposing scientific hypotheses and making predictions. This tradition has an essential influence even on modern education in China.

Like education, the development of libraries benefited from the creation of the earliest writing system. The first libraries were imperial libraries that collected royal records and served only the government. Private book collectors appeared with the Hundred Schools of Thought, when individual scholars published and built up their own collections. They were owned and managed by literate élites, including famous scholars and editorial appraisers with an enthusiasm for preserving culture, family legacy and local history. The privately owned libraries were mostly destroyed during the reign of Qin Shi Huang, and were revitalized in the following Han dynasty. After that both government-owned and private libraries systems coexisted for many centuries.

Collection growth throughout the entire classical era was in a pattern of spiral development. Every dynasty change was accomplished with military force accompanied by vast destruction of the properties of the previous empire in order for the successor to show its legitimacy. Library collections, particularly imperial ones, were among such destroyed properties, because successors claimed that they were 'immoral'. There were at least a dozen major library demolitions in history, each of which was catastrophic to library collections. Similarly, private libraries also had difficulties escaping damage in war-ridden years. Nonetheless, in spite of these harmful incidents, every type of library could be restored each time after a major destruction, serving to transmit and preserve an enormous array of historical heritage for the country.

Library collection management became standardized in the Han dynasty when Liu Xiang and Liu Xin drafted a book that set up a classification system for all collections (Zhang, 2003: 2). This first bibliographical book, *Qi Lue* (*Seven Outlines*), classifies all books into seven categories: history, scholars, arts, literature, military, science and technology. The book was also the first to record the total number of items (33,090 volumes) in the government library. Thereafter, research on bibliographic control consumed many human and material resources in almost every dynasty, creating and maturing a unique system of classification (dominated by four categories – classics, history, scholars and collections – to replace the seven categories) for the organization of libraries lasting almost two millennia.

The publishing industry experienced changes that reflected technological and political conditions. Prior to the introduction of printing technologies, scholars recorded their works on different types of material, making mass production impossible. This individualized publishing lacked necessary standards and therefore muddled the learned society. Collating publications thus became a custom in scholarly publishing; and top scholars teamed together for collation in almost every dynasty even after printing had been introduced. Many of the famous historical books were the results of such collations. When printing technologies appeared, there were several levels of publishing models: central and local governments operated official publishing houses (at the peak time of publishing development, every government agency had its own publishing house); publishing workshops were privately owned for commercial purposes; and family-based publishing existed not for commercial use and was made possible by wealthy scholars who could sustain the costs.

It is interesting to note that although in general scholarly conduct during the classical era was limited by governments to the pursuit of humanities, books in other areas were also published widely and were actually better preserved than books in the humanities. Government libraries collected books on medicine, mathematics, astronomy, hydrology, agriculture, technology and so on. Officials tolerated the publication of such materials because they were non-threatening to the government, in contrast to humanities publications that might potentially contain dangerous thoughts. New dynasties were more likely to keep the non-humanities books of the preceding dynasty because these did not usually carry the ideology of the past monarchs. This tolerance and encouragement enabled the accumulation of a great deal of historical manuscripts covering virtually every scholarly subject, and this adds to our understanding of scholarly communication in history.

Modern enlightenment (the late nineteenth century to 1949)

Several incidents interrupted Chinese scholarly tradition, which had been developed and pursued for more than 2,000 years. Beginning with the Opium War (1840–1842), Western countries defeated the corrupted Qing regime several times and forced China to open its doors to the world. Western influence penetrated many aspects of Chinese society, both technological and scholarly, so that modernity was conceived in various dimensions. After the Qing dynasty was brought down by a bourgeois revolution, the political situation was characterized by chaos and a weak central power that experienced successive changes from muddled warlordism to unstable republican hegemony, Japanese invasion and civil war until the communists established a strong rule in 1949. Like other periods of decentralized politics in history, this modern era observed political tolerance of scholarly freedom, albeit limited, in academia. It is therefore not surprising to see a large variety of Western thoughts and ideas, some of which were politically sensitive, in the publications of the time. It is also not surprising that a mixture of research methods and theories flourished in many academic areas.

The more intellectuals were exposed to the rational West thought that was introduced, the more they were frustrated by the tradition rooted in Chinese history. They struggled with balancing social reforms and the maintenance of national identity. The outcome of the struggle was the May Fourth Movement in 1919, started by college students and scholars to re-evaluate Chinese cultural institutions such as Confucianism and advocate the significance of science and technology for the prosperity of the country – 'Mr Morality and Mr Science'. The impact of the movement on the development of modern scholarly communication in China was unprecedented, e.g. the reform of written Chinese. Prior to the movement the written language was classical Chinese, which was designed only for highly educated people and was difficult to write and read. A new form of written language, vernacular Chinese, which was very close to the structure and vocabulary of the spoken language, became predominant and brought scholarly exchange to a broader audience.

Fundamental changes to the educational system included the termination of the civil service exam, *ke ju*, and the establishment of a Western model of education. A reorganization of the system began a modern structure of primary, secondary and tertiary education. Science, technology, medicine and world cultures were brought to each level of the curriculum, parallel to traditional subjects such as literature and history. For the first time textbooks written using a US or UK model in both content and style were introduced to schools and students at all levels, covering traditional as well as non-traditional curriculum materials. Well-edited texts and beautiful illustrations entertained while educating students. The use of the textbooks helped standardize nationwide teaching and learning and brought new generations to the panorama of global culture and nature.

One of the first college institutions was founded by the USA through war indemnity incurred after the invasion of the Eight-Nation Alliance (Britain, Japan, Russia, Italy, Germany, France, the USA and Australia). Jing Shi Da Xue Tang (the Imperial University of Peking) was the predecessor of Peking University that initiated the May Fourth Movement, and became a symbol of academic freedom in China up to the present day. At the beginning, Peking University comprised six schools – arts, sciences, law, medicine, engineering and agriculture – as well as a research institute for the humanities. To some extent the funding by the USA helped facilitate the implementation of American-style schooling, not only for Peking University but also for all higher educational institutions that followed.

In conjunction with the ground-breaking new educational and learning system, a revolution occurred in the government libraries, including fundamental changes to collection development and management, and most importantly to public services. Unlike previous libraries that only opened their doors to the élites, libraries at this time began serving a great array of readers, including scholars and the general public. Library collections also contained materials from other countries. Moreover, classification systems from the West, especially the USA, such as the Dewey Decimal System and Library of Congress Classification, were introduced and modified by consulting with traditional Chinese classifications to meet the needs of contemporaneous collections. An American librarian and philanthropist, Mary Elizabeth Wood, founded the first modern public library in Wuhan, Hubei province, which opened to the public in 1910. She also raised funds to create the first library school in China and even sent students to study library science in the USA. Because of her tireless efforts, American influence was important in the growth and development of Chinese libraries and librarianship.

One of the first modern libraries was the Capital Library, established by the central republic government in Nanjing in 1912. By the early 1930s there were 109 libraries of this type at both national and local levels, operated by government agencies and private universities, with a total of an estimated 4 million volumes. Even Chairman Mao of the succeeding communists once worked as an assistant at Peking University's library. Some libraries launched a partnership with libraries in the West, e.g. a scholarly exchange program between the National Peking Library and Columbia University Library. Most made great efforts to promote research activities, and published research articles as well as journals and bulletins for general information.

Publishing multiplied with the introduction of mass-printing machines from the West. In addition to books, journals and newspapers proliferated and impacted on the social life of the Chinese, both scholars and the general public. Many publishing houses were operated by modern-style management and were even incorporated. Among these publishing houses, Shang Wu Yin Shu Guan (Commercial Press, 1897) and Zhong Hua Shu Ju (China Publishing House, 1912) were best known for publishing numerous academic books, and have continued their business operations up to the present day. Both are giant business enterprises in the publishing industry with branches in major Chinese and overseas cities, and both employ many top scholars to edit, author and translate books and dictionaries.

The first law for publication by the republic government was established in the early twentieth century, claiming to grant citizens the freedom of press, assembly and speech. Both the Publication Law and the Copyright Law were passed in 1927. Although the interpretation and implementation of these laws varied because of the unstable political situation at the time, their appearance indicated the beginning of a different epoch for the publishing industry. Since then, scholarly communication has had a new look.

Planned economy (1949–1977)

With the founding of the People's Republic of China in 1949, the Communist Party established a strong rule over the country, and Hong Kong and Taiwan became estranged from the system for political reasons. The Korean War left China aloof from Western countries, while a long relationship with the former Soviet Union led China to a planned economy as opposed to a market economy. Everything became planned, not only the economy but also scholarly conduct. For about three decades diversity gave place to homogeneity – to the extent that even the vocabulary used by researchers in their studies was programmed.

Politically and socially, the country entered a stage of collectivism where individual thoughts were restricted and intellectual inspirations were suppressed. The situation was highlighted and worsened by continual political campaigns aiming to empower one voice. As a result scholarly creativity was curbed, particularly in the social sciences and humanities, where alternate expressions could be in conflict with the ideology of the government. At its worst during the Cultural Revolution (1966–1976), when government censorship was everywhere, only a few academic fields that did not study contemporary subjects, such as archaeology and history, retained certain levels of research activity. However, even this had to serve the cause of political propaganda, and the less politically sensitive fields were not totally immune from the influence of a planned economy. Scholarly interests conceded to social and government demands where research allocations in science, engineering and medicine were concerned. For a long time, decision-making for research infrastructure was in the hands of communist non-scholars. At the same time, lacking effective and efficient communication with peers both domestically and abroad impeded the healthy progress of scientific investigations.

Under the planned economy, Chinese universities were restructured in the early 1950s. Major changes included moving from private to public ownership, i.e. all universities started to be operated by different levels of government – either the central government or provincial and municipal governments; and moving from research to subject-based institutions, e.g. social sciences and the humanities were separated from engineering to become independent entities, while agriculture, mining, forestry, teaching, medicine etc. were all on their own. This second change reshaped the pedagogical foundations, with significant influence up to the most recent years: students in professional schools were not required to take basic courses in arts and sciences.

University teachers and students were an unfortunate group. Their bad luck began with the anti-rightist movement in 1957 that accused top intellectuals of promoting pluralism of expression and criticism of the government. Then, in 1966, when Chairman Mao launched the Cultural Revolution to solicit more power, students were utilized as tools – the Red Guards – to create massive social, cultural, political and economic chaos. Later, both students and teachers were blamed and sent to the countryside to 'learn from the peasants'. Universities ceased operation for several years, and education was brought to a complete halt. When teachers stopped instruction and students ceased studying, scholarly communication was inevitably interrupted at the beginning of a cycle that involves learning, creating, publicizing and disseminating information and knowledge. Consequently, the entire communication system was affected. It is thus not surprising to observe a very slow development of every aspect of scholarly communication during the Cultural Revolution in China, although the sluggishness was not necessarily the theoretical outcome of a planned economy.

Ever since the Communist Party took over the country, it had made efforts to control and regulate book production, distribution and price. These efforts were well documented in the transition of the publishing industry from mostly private owned to exclusively government owned. Publishing houses such as Shang Wu Yin Shu Guan and Zhong Hua Shu Ju were first forced to share a partnership with the government, and were then totally converted into public properties. The publication of scholarly work became the business of government-run publishers, by no means independent from the influence of concurrent policies and political preferences which represented the government's intent. Financial profit was no longer the purpose of any publishers, whose budget deficits would be paid by and whose budget surplus would be supplied to the government. Without motivation to develop, the industry became disadvantageous to scholars. At the same time, publication prices were set according to print quantities, which was another reason why it was difficult for scholarly work to be published.

All publications were distributed to readers through the Xinhua Bookstore, a state-owned store chain with thousands of outlets in every corner of the country. When the communist government was first established there were almost 200 private book distributors. Six years later the Xinhua Bookstore became the only one, and was instrumental in promoting governmental policies and distributing cultural, scientific and technological information. Like publishers, the Xinhua Bookstore was a not-for-profit organization that had government sponsorship: it lacked incentives to seek expansion and thus lacked interest in marketing publications and broadening readership among researchers and the general public.

A planned economy was theorized to harness land, labor and capital to serve the economic objectives of a country and maximize the continuous utilization of all available resources without suffering the effects of a business cycle. Its implementation in China achieved neither goal: poor economic planning incurred severe costs in the development of industry and agriculture. With regard to scholarly communication, an inefficient and ineffective system obstructed scholarly innovations and publishing, which can easily be proved by a simple comparison of publication figures between this time period and beforehand. Unquestionably, heavy political intervention was partially responsible. The fiercest political campaign of the Communist Party – the Cultural Revolution – accelerated this intervention and damaged the centrally planned economy, and all aspects of scholarly activities were reduced to a minimum for more than a decade.

Reforms and opening up (1977–2001)

In the year 1978 universities greeted the first two classes of students admitted after a decade-long closure of the educational system. The society was in great need of trained talent for its economic and technological revitalization. As one of a series of symbolic changes that the new leader Deng Xiaoping brought to the country, China ended its planned economy and embarked on the road to economic reforms and openness. Several milestone policies were conceived to deregulate the government's control of the industrial sector and introduce market competition to the economy. The country was at this point described as standing over the so-called 'debris' of an economy, culture and educational system that had been smashed by the Cultural Revolution. Everything needed to be recovered through reforms.

Reforms have since created an economic miracle for the country. For almost 30 consecutive years there has been a tenfold increase in GDP, which recently made China the fourth-largest economic power in the world. In early 2007 China officially announced itself as the second-largest economy by domestic PPP (purchasing power parity), measured at about US$10 trillion. Such rapid development helped drop the poverty rate from more than 50 per cent of the population at the beginning of the reforms to about 8 per cent in the new millennium. Overall, the transition from a centrally planned economy to a more market-oriented economy has been very easy. More than 70 per cent of GDP is created in the private sector, although state enterprises still control utilities, energy resources and some heavy industries. At this point, the average Chinese person is able to enjoy higher living standards in terms of personal income, consumer spending and life expectancy.

Together with the continuous leap forward in the national economy, information and communications technology (ICT) ballooned due to the advances in computing and technology in the last two decades. Since its first internet connection in 1987, China had reached 137 million internet users by December 2006, representing approximately 11 per cent of internet users in the world. About 66 per cent of them use broadband. At the peak expansion period between 1997 and 2002, the telecommunication sector had a growth rate of 20 per cent. The rapid development of ICT penetrated every aspect of scholarly communication and brought a revolution to the creation, evaluation, distribution and preservation of information and knowledge.

Socially and culturally, China's door was wide open to the world. China faced profound challenges as well as opportunities. Increased scholarly exchanges and research collaborations between the Chinese and their foreign colleagues helped facilitate their understanding of each other. China's scholarly communication system gradually changed from a model similar to that of the former Soviet Union to a model resembling the West, particularly the USA, although the uniqueness of its tradition was still retained.

If 'prosperity' describes the outcomes of the reform and open-door policy since the late 1970s, 'eager for fast development' best characterizes the attitudes of the entire country towards playing catch-up economically and technologically with the developed countries, and of average people in every aspect of their lives. Encouraged by government policies, people look for rapid changes that can bring maximum profits instantly. Anxiety for fast growth became contagious, spreading all over the place. As a result, changes at all levels were designed and executed to target immediate results, as opposed to undergoing a solid social and cultural construction for longer-term development. And the pressure for financial profit influenced the conduct of scholarly communication.

Higher education

Universities were in their heyday at the beginning of the reforms, when higher education resumed operation after a decade-long pause. The values of knowledge were recognized again, in comparison with past decades when scholars had been placed at the lowest level of the social hierarchy by a series of political sanctions. Universities were again the center of attention of society as a place to deliver knowledge, breed intellectuals and educate a group of specially selected students. Students wishing to attend a university were required to sit a competitive entrance exam: less than 4 per cent of the total high school graduates nationwide were admitted. Thus acceptance basically guaranteed a bright future with great honor, since all graduates would be assigned a good job by the government. It was the dream of every student to receive higher education.

Both students and professors were enthusiastic about learning and teaching. It was typical that students waited for a long time outside university libraries and classrooms before the buildings even opened in order to get a seat. For the first few years colleges allowed both students graduating from high school and previous graduates to take the national entrance examination. As a result, these years had students of mixed ages. The mature students had much incentive to study and were able to manage their schedule well. They were also lucky to be instructed and supervised by top scholars who otherwise might have concentrated on their own research instead of teaching undergraduate courses.

Soon, graduate-level training was incorporated into higher education. Not only universities but also research institutions and top libraries were approved to offer masters degrees. The latter two, with strong disciplinary research strengths, are still granting graduate degrees today. For more than a decade educational programs were principally tailored to the needs of bachelors and masters, so when doctoral education was first introduced many programs had no more to offer than a language course and a political course, the latter being the remnants of a Soviet model.

Administratively, all universities were under the leadership of the ministries of education at the national or provincial levels, and also co-managed by another government agency. For example, Peking University reported to both the State Education Ministry (now the State Education Commission) and the City of Beijing, and Beijing Agricultural University was managed by the State Ministries of Education and Agriculture. These co-sponsors had the authority to allocate funding and decide policies, while universities were responsible for providing quality education and scientific research by creating proper teaching plans and curricula and encouraging faculty to make active contributions to research. Faculty, once hired, were ensured a lifelong stable job and could not be laid off according to their working performance – a tenure status called *tie fan wan* (iron rice bowl), extended from the planned economy. At the beginning of the reforms, students, as before, did not have much freedom to select courses and subjects but had to follow a specific curriculum. Both faculty and students received a benefits package from the university. For faculty the package covered health, pension and housing; for students it included free tuition and accommodation, plus a small stipend to defray their family's financial burden.

The glory of higher education did not last long, and quick economic progress in other areas stole the thunder of the universities. Students and professors started to feel neglected by the government, since educational allocations and their personal incomes were lower than those in other modernization programs. Dissatisfaction with injustice and with corruption by certain political leaders fermented on campuses, leading to a series of demonstrations in Tiananmen Square in Beijing in spring 1989, and driving additional reforms for higher education.

Beginning in the late 1980s, a series of education reforms initiated numerous changes in administration and adjusted educational opportunity, direction and content. Universities became more independent in making decisions on personnel, budget and other infrastructure changes. Some changes had visible results in the reshaping of Chinese education. First, universities were allowed to raise money from various sources, including tuition that was once free for students. Although still not-for-profit in status, higher educational institutions had to generate sufficient income to cover the expenses not paid by the government, including bonuses to make employee salaries compatible with other professions and expansions to keep abreast of educational competition. Universities were not isolated from a market society where everyone was seeking high-speed development. Consequently, students and parents saw a frequent tuition race and constantly enlarged enrollments. The admission rate skyrocketed from less than 4 per cent of applicants in the late 1970s to nearly 60 per cent, with a total of 8.67 million applicants in 2007 (Ministry of Education, 2007). But the expansion of university facilities lagged far behind the increase in student enrollments; furthermore, the market was not prepared to provide enough jobs for college graduates. It became graduates' responsibility to find employment, rather than being assigned jobs by the government. Each year more than one-third of students cannot find a job within six months of graduation.

Such a high unemployment rate triggered the expansion of graduate education, as a great number of bachelor degree holders chose to advance to masters' studies in order to avoid the immediate frustrations of job-hunting. However, soon the masters' holders too started to face difficulties, and many continued on to get a doctorate. By the new millennium China had become the second leading country, after only the USA, in granting PhD degrees. This great leap forward did not come without a price: the questionable quality of higher training. When there were not enough faculty members to supervise students and when faculty became bound more tightly to research than teaching, mass production of doctorates was by no means a positive outcome of the educational reforms.

Second, the tenure structure for faculty was deeply shaken by reforms that aimed to smash their *tie fan wan*. A new system reappointed professors based on regular evaluations of their academic levels and performance, usually for two to four years at a time. Though evaluation criteria varied from institution to institution, they typically favored research in the forms of publication and grants. Most institutions set threshold numbers for scholarly publications and valued peer-reviewed articles in top journals, particularly international journals, more than others. Such evaluations had been proven effective in the practice of many developed countries and thus should work well in China. In reality, however, the Chinese versions of evaluation ignored special conditions such as teaching-oriented colleges and the overall heavy instructional load of professors in ever-expanding universities. The strict quantitative requirements of publication were fulfilled in many cases at the sacrifice of publication quality and instructional competence.

The reform also failed to deal with a common issue of unfairness in college admissions that set different selection standards by geographic locations. Each year, the State Education Commission decided the minimum scores required for acceptance, which fluctuated significantly from province to province. It was more difficult for students in densely populated regions to get into a college than for those in less populated and remote areas. Cities where universities were abundant, such as Beijing and Shanghai, were exceptions. This issue receives less attention now because of the overall increase in college admissions all over the country.

And third, private enterprises were initially tolerated, and then legitimized, to participate in educational ventures. Compared to public universities, they have more flexibility in administration and setting up programs and curricula. But they are relatively new and have not been able to reach a size comparable to the public universities; and almost all of them have only designed professional programs to satisfy the market without immediate plans to boost research activities. However, their participation symbolizes a privatization process in education and could have considerable impact on future higher training.

Publishing – monographs

The planned economy left a very unproductive publishing industry in the country. In 1979 only 17,212 book titles were published, including both scholarly and general types of materials (Publishers Association of China, 1980: 612). It had been difficult for everyone – authors and publishers to publish work, bookstores to sell and readers to buy books. Readers enthusiastically looked forward to new books, particularly when the value of knowledge was recognized by society and trained talents were in enormous demand after the Cultural Revolution. Reforms held great potential for the development of a prolific publishing industry.

Privatization has been the main theme of reforms over the years. Nonetheless, privatization in the publishing industry was not straightforward and could be portrayed as a process of semi-privatization. This was the product of a strange combination of the economic freedom and political restrictions in the country. Even though the publishing industry was an integral part of the market economy, the government adamantly refused to withdraw its firm control so as to maintain the necessary political censorship. The first step of privatization in the publishing industry happened in the system of book distribution in the late 1970s. For ten years until 1977, when universities reopened their doors to students, high school graduates had been sent by the government to the countryside to be peasants. Only a few could now compete with graduating high school students to pass the entrance examinations in order to get into a college. The rest were allowed by the government to return to their home cities. All of a sudden, cities were full of unemployed youngsters who had missed their higher education training and were not able to find an immediate job with their farming skills. They were encouraged by the government to go into self-employment in professions that were not permitted previously under the planned economy, mostly in services such as retailing. For the first time after almost three decades, small-scale bookselling broke the monopoly of the Xinhua Bookstore.

Some documents about the reform of the book distribution system by the State Bureau of Publication were responses by the government to individuals' participation in retailing publications (Publishers Association of China, 1981, 1983). The documents suggested policy changes to encourage a diversity of sources of investment and operational strategies in publication distribution and the shortening of the distribution cycle. Although only focusing on retailing, these documents were the first official statements that authorized a privatization of publishing. Alongside a series of other new policies in the subsequent years, they stimulated the process of privatization. Instantaneously, private investment mushroomed in the publishing industry, and reached its peak in the mid-1990s.

In past decades the Xinhua Bookstore had controlled nationwide bookselling, wholesale and retail. Its private competitors now began to play a dominant role in both areas. A rapidly developing wholesale market, supervised by the government, was occupied actively by small-sized wholesalers that had developed from the early book retailers. Publishing houses soon joined the wholesale venture when they were granted permission to bypass the Xinhua Bookstore and go directly to market. Nowadays a dynamic wholesale business supports the circulation of publications. Likewise, privatization became noticeable in the retailing business, where large-scale private bookstores humiliated the Xinhua Bookstore by supplying more books in both quantity and type and providing a much better purchasing and reading environment. For example, a private bookstore in Beijing was able to display more than 200,000 book titles at its opening in the late 1990s, and many other bookstores offered more than 150,000 books at a time. By contrast, the Xinhua Bookstore lingered on in a steadily worsening condition, and would hardly have survived were it not for the sale of elementary and middle school textbooks.

In reality, privatization was never truly restricted to bookselling only. It found ways to creep into book publishing, starting in the early 1980s – a public secret that was tolerated by the government so long as the content of publications was not politically threatening and was morally acceptable by society. Up to the late 1990s private publishers were able to produce more than half of all the new books on the market. Among other strategies, purchasing ISBNs (International Standard Book Numbers) from a state-owned publishing house was a relatively common way for a private publisher to participate in publishing. Although officially prohibited from trading ISBNs, publishers were always able to figure out a way. Another strategy was buying the title of a state-owned publishing house in order to print books legally and pursue financial benefits in an indirect way. At the same time, some managed to secure their businesses by partnering with state-owned publishers through affiliating a for-profit entity to a non-profit organization or co-publishing books with the latter.

This was a win-win situation for every party. The government lost nothing but financial and management burdens of supporting a non-profitable publishing system. The risk of political threats could be minimized by taking control of ISBNs and governmental intervention in retailing. Public publishers made money from doing business with their private colleagues, which helped ease financial hardship resulting from a decrease in government subsidy, and also satisfied the duty of publishing scholarly materials that always had a small market. Readers and private publishers were the biggest beneficiaries in this relationship. The former benefited from having a great array of selections, while the latter, because of their close contact with the market as well as their flexibility in operations, raked in immense profits from printing and selling popular books. It is said that publishing was then one of the most profitable industries, next to only electronic information, manufacturing and tourism (Zheng, 2004). Private publishers received the bigger part of the profit pie.

The growth of publishers and publications was phenomenal in this time period. As a snapshot illustrating the growth rates, the number of new publications increased dramatically from about 13,000 book titles in 1977 to 96,761 titles in 1993 and 170,962 titles in 2002; the number of book sales nearly quadrupled from 1,253,949 volumes in 1993 to 4,349,307 in 2002; and the number of periodical titles nearly doubled from 3,415 in 1983 to 7,011 in 1993. These figures do not include audio-video materials, electronic resources or newspapers. The number of state-owned publishing houses jumped from 114 in 1977 to 566 in 1999; and private publishers totalled more than 3,500 by the end of the 1990s (Publishers Association of China, 1984: 158, 1994: 14).

Both public and private publishing houses published scholarly work, although each had its own focus. Private houses liked to select classic scholarly work, both domestic and foreign, as well as textbook-assisting materials. Despite the fact that financial pursuits were obviously their primary goal, most of their owners and managers were formerly scholars who occasionally produced research work of high quality so as not to be regarded as too commercially greedy. For public houses, including general publishers, university presses and publishers for special professions, the production of scholarly work was their assigned duty. They contributed and would continue to contribute more scholarly books to the research community than their private competitors.

If new books published with ISBNs were grouped into several general categories, the largest category covered books under the topics of culture, education and sports – more than one-third of the entire monographic output. One-fifth of titles were science and technology books. The third-largest group was economics books, forming about one-tenth of new publications.

A privatization process, though in different forms, was undertaken by all state-run publishing houses as part of necessary reforms. On the one hand they carried a heavy burden of personnel costs left by the planned economy; and on the other hand they experienced severe budget cuts from the government. However, in return they were granted a more independent status that allowed them to make their own decisions and be less obligated to the government. The publishers worked to adjust to the emergent challenges. Major changes included partnering with one (or more) private publisher that would potentially bring in money, selecting popular products that might be able to attract a larger group of readers and organizing their own wholesale and retail structure to save unnecessary waste in distribution. Most publishers also gave high priority to publishing books that might be compensated by sponsorship through authors or other agents.

The publication of scholarly books also benefited from a policy change that allowed books to be priced according to their actual cost. Previously, under the planned economy, book prices were set lower than their production cost and only brought in profits for publishers if the print quantity was very high. Scholarly materials were typically printed in small quantities and frequently suffered under the old pricing policy. Since 1980 the government had set a cap for pricing and periodically raised the cap limit, so academic publishers could have relatively free control over the pricing of their publications, except for textbooks for K–12 (kindergarten to twelfth grade) students.

Under such a publishing situation, research work with practical potential was preferred to basic and pure theoretical work. Moreover, the quality of publications might be questioned if financial considerations were very much involved in the selection of titles. This commercial influence on scholarly communication mirrored a capitalist society where the attitude of regular citizens towards seeking money had changed cultural values. Behind the prosperity of the publishing industry lay serious concerns about a lost tradition, although some might debate the level of seriousness.

Publishing – journals

There were several hundred periodicals at the beginning of the economic reforms. This figure reached nearly 9,000 by the late 1990s, including both scholarly journals and popular magazines. It was estimated that about 4,000 were scholarly journals (Publishers Association of China, 2000: 74–5; Wu et al., 2004). These journals were managed, edited and printed by professional associations, universities, state-owned publishing houses and other academic organizations or governmental agencies. All must be authorized by the State News and Publishing Office and other ministries or commissions. Private publishers did not invest a lot in scholarly journals, partly because the government discouraged privatization in this part of the publishing industry, and partly because such journals were not financially rewarding.

Despite the rapid expansion in their numbers, the operational style of the journals at first followed to some extent what was practiced under the planned economy. The sponsoring institution of a journal provided financial support plus necessary space and facilities, and also assigned personnel. Traditional operation was characterized by a unique review and editing process for an average journal – a three-tier system instead of peer review. This three-tier structure contained a hierarchy of editors, senior editors and editor-in-chief. Initial screening of submitted articles was carried out at the bottom of the hierarchy, while at the top the editor-in-chief made the final decision on publication. A quasi-peer-review process slowly evolved in many journals, inviting senior scholars in relevant academic fields to review selected articles. Recommendations from the review were respected by journals, but were only adopted if they did not conflict with the opinions of the three-tier editors. Nonetheless, reviewers played a more important role in recommending topics and contributors to journals.

Such a three-tier decision system was one of the reasons why many articles of low research quality could get published. All editors were full-time journal employees who were not required to be involved in scientific research, and therefore might have very limited knowledge about the most recent research developments. In many cases the journals hired personnel based on their language skills as opposed to their contributions to the profession which the journal was serving. To solve this problem, many journals have gradually brought in editors with professional training in related areas and at least a master's or preferably a doctoral degree. This change, however, was still not enough to solve the problem, because the new editors would also find it impossible to keep abreast of research progress without actively participating in any research projects.

The editorial review system was not the only reason for the publication of numerous unqualified papers in academic journals. Since scholars were under enormous pressure from a competitive system that required endless evaluations, where the evaluations were closely linked to income level and even employment, a few people decided to risk their reputation by cheating on publications. Both plagiarism and manipulating scientific data burgeoned. Extreme cases of plagiarism included entire articles being copied and submitted for publication to another journal with only changes in authors' names. Alternatively, the same author might send one of his/her published articles to a different journal without making changes. Many incidents of publication plagiarism have been discovered, and consequent punishments have ranged from only a warning to terminating employment. Comparatively, the manipulation of research data is more difficult to detect.

Recently, when budget cuts were unavoidable by most journals in all state-owned publishing houses, advertising became the primary way of supplementing reduced revenue, and a pay-to-publish model was also experimented with and actually incorporated into the publication cycle of some journals. Pay-to-publish helped journals bring in money and at the same time worked well for certain authors who could *buy* publication opportunities: scholars who did not have research agendas and articles of competitive quality, but who might have access to resources. Their ability to afford publication fees gave them advantages over others regardless of the quality of their articles. This opportunity was mostly available in low-ranked journals, such as those published by small universities.

Advertising was crucial for most scholarly journals. In addition to inserting advertisements into regular issues, many journals published special issues for particular sponsors in return for money. To regulate the publication of special issues, the government set policies allowing only one per year. It was a common practice for research journals to attempt to cut costs by shortening or eliminating references in published articles to give space to advertisements. This practice was criticized extensively for causing a major hurdle for researchers to find related readings and make proper citations, and also for providing a convenience to plagiarists.

It was generally not easy for journals to achieve economic self-sufficiency given the further fact that journals themselves did not control the subscription process. All domestic distributions were made through the News and Periodical Post Office, which charged each journal 20–40 per cent of the subscription. Overseas subscriptions were managed by the China International Book Trading Corporation. Furthermore, most journals were cheap in retail price in order to compete in the market; and many academic journals have a tradition of paying authors for their contribution, based mostly on the length of the article. China was a paradise for authors, who earned not only academic visibility but also money from publishing articles in scholarly journals.

Journals had different levels of scholarly quality. This is normal when fast journal expansion is taken into account. Seeking quantity might naturally have the negative consequence of having to surrender quality. Fortunately, many top-ranked journals published high-quality research articles and played an important role in supporting a healthy system of scholarly communication. These journals usually had a long history and were managed and edited by professional associations or famous research institutions at the national or provincial level. Peking University compiled a list of such core journals that was widely recognized by scholars and students (Calvert and Shi, 2001). Journals with high status attracted more readers and thus had a higher circulation, which generated more revenue. This would drive the journal editors to ensure better quality of published articles.

At the other end of the spectrum was a group of university journals. Except for some well-known universities that managed quality journals, many lesser-known universities had struggled with economic as well as scholarly pursuits. Academically, these journals faced two problems in management. First, such a journal served an entire university community with totally different academic disciplines, ranging from social sciences to sciences, technology and medicine. The editorial board obviously lacked the necessary knowledge to judge articles on these diverse subjects. Second, many of the universities employed a mixed group of faculty who were either too busy teaching to conduct research or did not have adequate training and qualifications to complete a good research article. Economically, since these journals published mostly low-quality articles they were not able to attract readers and had a low circulation in the first place. The unfavorable situation forced their editors to seek alternatives to boost their development, such as asking authors to pay for publishing – which unfortunately creates a vicious publishing cycle, because this pay-to-publish model may easily bring in low-quality articles. Future reforms must either reorganize the structure or keep only those journals that are in good shape.

Libraries

Much like the renaissance of higher education and publishing, under the reforms and open-door policy libraries have enjoyed a fruitful period since the late 1970s. Unlike the publishing industry, that was redirected by a privatization process, libraries experienced their remarkable recovery and expansion with support from the government at various levels in their policy changes and financial needs. This development was necessary to provide services to the modernizing national economy and the restoration of social and cultural values.

As early as the 1980s, the central government emphasized the importance of improving the services of libraries and information resources. A number of policies were issued and councils and commissions were founded to regulate varied types of libraries in every area of their development in response to immense shortages in library building space, collection sizes and qualified personnel. Within a couple of years the number of libraries had significantly expanded. For example, in 1985 there were over 2,300 public libraries, more than double the number in 1978; and there were more than 1,000 academic libraries, in comparison to about 130 a few years previously. Not only had the size of libraries been enlarged, but library facilities and collection development had also been improved. For example, by the mid-1980s the total collections of academic and public libraries numbered 6 billion volumes, double the size in 1978; and by the late 1990s the total number reached 10 billion volumes (Huang, 1987: 40, 42, Tables 3, 6; Lin, 2005: Table 1.8).

Libraries at this time could be categorized into public, academic, school and special libraries, as well as information or documentation centers. Public libraries were supported by the central and local governments and built in almost every city. Among them, the National Library of China and Shanghai (Municipal) Library were the largest in both building space and collections. Academic libraries, represented by Peking University Library, served the teaching, research and learning needs of university faculty and students, while school libraries were only available in large middle or high schools in major cities. Special libraries were among the fastest-growing types of libraries. They were joined by information and documentation centers to serve readers with special needs.

The National Library of China (NLC) is the only national library in mainland China. It was previously known as Beijing Library; the name was changed officially in 1998. It is a public library as well as a comprehensive research library serving the central legislature, government, key research institutions and businesses. With the purpose of implementing the official cultural agreements and conducting communication and cooperation with libraries both at home and abroad, it plays a central role in the development of library standardization and automation. By the late 1990s it had a floor space of 140,000 square meters and a collection of more than 20 million volumes, making it the fifth-largest library in the world. Its more than 30 reading rooms have 3,000 seats and receive 7,000–8,000 readers a day. Its strong Chinese collections cover manuscripts of revolutionary historical materials, doctoral dissertations and UN publications, in addition to a rapidly increasing number of e-publications. The library also houses the biggest collection of materials in foreign languages in the country (Library Society of China, 2006).

Peking University Library, with a history of more than 100 years, is one of the major libraries in the country. It has a collection of over

6 million items, making it the largest academic library in Asia. The library now has a floor space of 54,000 square meters and more than 4,000 reading seats serving faculty and students of the university. It is famous for a large rare book collection and numerous historical documents. It has played a pivotal role in recent digitization developments in academic libraries all over the country by collaborating with state-run digital projects and other educational and cultural institutions (Peking University Library, 2007).

However, the expansion of libraries was always unable to catch up with the growth of the national economy and could not satisfy the needs of society. It was very common for the reading rooms of a library – academic, public and others – to be full of readers at all times. Hence a university library was usually only accessible by its own students and faculty with a valid ID. Similarly, many public libraries such as the NLC only issued a library loan card to researchers at the level of assistant professor and above, and to government officials above a designated rank. Except for current periodicals and newspapers, regular stacks in most libraries were not open to readers, who would have to obtain a book by providing bibliographic information to a circulation librarian. This created a heavy workload for librarians on the one hand, and lengthened book-locating time for readers on the other. A response to the difficulty of library usage was the flourishing of small independent reading rooms operated by individual organizations, although they had very limited collections.

Another challenge that all libraries faced at the beginning of the reforms was a severe shortage of qualified librarians. Libraries used to be a place where people of incompetence in other positions were relocated, because library jobs had been stereotyped as being easy to handle. Such a negative image of librarians limited people's reliance on libraries to discover information, but was progressively corrected by employing more and more professionally educated library graduates.

With economic fluctuations in the reform process, libraries were not exempt from financial crises caused by irregular budget cuts and regular price increases for publications. Besides operating in the most cost-effective way, many libraries began charging a fee for certain services, particularly services for business and technological information closely connected to the commercial and industrial sectors. Most libraries, though themselves not-for-profit in nature, organized a subordinate unit to make profits on providing information consultancy so as to balance their budget deficits. Such endeavors had surprising success due to the increasing demand for information caused by the growth of the economy and information technology after the mid-1990s. Profitable prospects enticed those who actually provided the consultation to break away from their libraries, making information consultancy an independent and expanding field that employed more than 1 million people by the late 1990s.

Libraries, especially academic, public and special libraries, played an active role in supporting scholarly communication. Their contributions were not limited to collection materials and reference help for research, which were traditional functions of libraries; many also contributed to scholarship by organizing a wide array of research activities such as conferences, lectures and workshops and launching cooperative research projects between libraries or between a library and another academic entity. The National Library of China alone, for example, held at least one lecture per day. Moreover, some libraries established publication exchange programs with domestic as well as international libraries to facilitate mutual understanding. For instance, as of the 1990s the NLC has an exchange relationship with more than 1,000 libraries and institutions around the world. Most recently, major libraries have joined the adventure of ICT development and have used digital platforms to preserve and disseminate scholarly information.

Digital communication

The advance of ICT had a fundamental impact on the innovation and development of digital communication. In the 1980s and early 1990s, CD-ROMs, microfilms, microfiches and tapes were the principal alternatives to preserving and presenting print materials. At the same time, library automation was planned, employed, tested and improved with the implementation of computer networks to facilitate online searching of library catalogs. When the internet became popular in the mid-1990s, Chinese information technology professionals, like their foreign colleagues, began the construction of internet resources to deliver information through the web.

From the beginning of this construction, digital projects were carried out under the guidance and support of the government. The earliest projects were primarily digital libraries that aimed at developing software applications, digitizing library collections and making them accessible on the internet. Library cooperation on digital projects was common in order to share technologies and resources. For instance, the China Pilot Digital Library project was a collaboration between the NLC and five public libraries – Shanghai, Shenzhen, Zhongshan, Liaoning and Nanjing – under the supervision of the State Culture Ministry. The earliest digital library projects included the China Pilot Digital Library, China National Knowledge Infrastructure, Chinese Academic Libraries & Information System, Peking University Digital Library and SuperStar Digital Library.

Online resources at an early stage contained several categories of digital content, including books, arts, gazetteers, historical documents, journals, newspapers and theses, focusing on preserving and publicizing Chinese historical heritage. All of the above-mentioned digital libraries had a large collection of historical materials, such as rubbings from ancient inscriptions and rare books. A large amount of historical archives were jointly published in digitized forms by archival societies at varied levels and publishing houses. Soon many digital libraries developed a burning interest in digitizing local gazetteers and genealogical documents. From 1979 to 1999 more than 10,000 gazetteers were published electronically by local governments at the provincial, municipal and county levels to trace local history (Zheng, 2004). Furthermore, the digitization of dissertations and theses became a major project by many digital libraries. The NLC and Peking University Library were the pioneers; and later many other research and academic libraries initiated their own thesis digitization projects.

Because of the limitation of technologies at this time, online search functions were not as flexible and reliable as in later years. Thus many electronic journals did not provide advanced searchability and could only be browsed by entire issues. E-journals were exclusively the digitized form of past journals and did not include electronic publishing of new journals, which became popular later on.

A couple of international collaborative projects were launched in the earliest digital efforts. Among others, the Dunhuang project was a joint venture between the British Library and the NLC to catalog and digitize a manuscript collection of the Silk Road (a series of trade routes starting from Xi'an, an ancient Chinese political and cultural center, and running through Asia Minor to the Mediterranean; for over 1,000 years it has functioned in connecting several major civilizations, including China, Egypt, India, Mesopotamia, Persia and Rome) preserved at the NLC; and the Chinese Memory Net project was made possible by both the Chinese and their American colleagues working with the support of the National Science Foundation in the USA. China also joined an international Million Books endeavor. Such global collaborations worked well in bringing Chinese digital efforts to international standards from the very beginning, so that worldwide sharing of data and information became possible. Many of the online resources were presented in both Chinese and English, making them widely readable. Technologically, most of the online materials were created with an international audience in mind; thus compatibility, such as file formats, and interoperability, such as metadata standards, were given serious consideration.

Internationalization (2001 onwards)

Since formally joining the WTO (World Trade Organization) in December 2001, China has begun another policy shift, readjusting the direction of the economy and other sectors of society. The government has since then initiated important guidelines to regulate the issues of equitable distribution of resources, and has been cautious about promoting merely the rate of growth. The previous two decades under the reforms and open-door policy had seen rapid progress in almost every aspect of society that provided wealth to scholarly communication, but at the same time raised problems of research misconduct, as shown above. Many people were concerned that the problems could negatively impact the foundation of the scholarly structure, and supported an appropriate reorientation.

From a historical perspective, this wealth of achievements in scholarly communication and accompanying disappointments are the logical products of a 'primitive accumulation of capital' (Marx, 1867) as part of large-scale market expansion. In order to survive modernization, commercialism has been irresistible to both scholars and organizations. Living in such an environment of money worship, the tendency to concentrate on quantity alone has come at the cost of letting quality go when both are competing for limited resources. However, 'accelerating reform' was the main theme of the Annual Sessions of the National People's Congress and the Chinese People's Political Consultative Conference in 2006; the sentence 'dilemmas caused by reforms can only be solved by further reforms' was first utilized by the government and then discussed by the public. Thus the process of scholarly communication can be readjusted through the efforts of authorities and ordinary researchers. Once prosperity has reached a comfortable level and 'capital' has accumulated considerably, people's attention will naturally shift to emphasizing quality – manifested, in the case of China, by attempts at facilitating internationalization and conforming to the world's standardization.

The internationalization attempts are symbolized, among other examples, by a restructuring of undergraduate curricula in higher learning, a further move to real peer review in journal publication, engagement of international businesses in the publishing industry, increasing emphasis on citation value, an incorporated enterprise in book distribution, intensified enforcement of copyright control and a digital campaign in information preservation and dissemination by libraries and other educational and cultural agencies. Even though most such efforts are now in their initial stages and may not be perfect, this tendency does represent an overall understanding of the issues created by a long-term quest for fast growth in the economy and the commercialized academic society. The following paragraphs highlight some of the internationalization attempts pertaining to the practice of scholarly communication.

Higher education

The restructuring of undergraduate curricula started in the late 1990s, when colleges with specializations were upgraded to universities. Within a couple of years, most colleges that were constructed under the planned economy in 1952 changed their names to universities. The name changes have to be approved by the State Education Commission and follow guidelines that include introducing arts and sciences training into the general curricula. Nationwide, numerous colleges of accounting, agriculture, architecture, forestry, geology, languages, mining, petroleum, textiles, trading, aerospace engineering, chemical industry, coal industry, posts and telecommunications and the like have now altered their titles to universities of engineering, industry, science or technology. At the same time, university merging is part of the upgrades. The most noticeable university merger is that the top-ranked Medical Science University of Beijing became the School of Medical Science in Peking University, which was its status in 1952 before the educational reorganization. Although it is still too early to evaluate if the name changes and university mergers are another type of a 'big leap forward' movement, they provide an opportunity for the majority, if not all, of higher educational institutions to readjust their teaching so that students can receive a broader training.

People's liking for ranking universities has increased in recent years. Several versions of university rankings have been created by universities or independent agents for different purposes. Among others, the ranking provided by Shanghai Jiao Tong University for world universities has received international recognition since 2003 because of its methodology, using many scientific measures. Although criticized in some aspects, this ranking emphasizes research contributions by faculty members, particularly in top-class journals such as *Science* and *Nature*, and links them to the prestige of a university. It represents people's increasing concern about the quality of higher academic training.

Publishing

It was not until very recently that a real peer-review system began to work in evaluating the quality of articles submitted to research journals. Although only leading journals have implemented this peer-review practice, editors have been increasingly aware of the importance of getting specialists involved in publication decisions. Scholars themselves also recognize the value of creating high-quality work and linking it to their career development. A broad range of efforts have been made to promote research, such as by enhancing its visibility through publishing in influential research journals, particularly internationally known journals, collaborating with foreign colleagues to conduct cutting-edge projects and highlighting the impact of article citations on major citation analyses. The efforts have been quite prolific. For example, according to the Science Citation Index, China produced only 4,880 recorded papers in 1987, but that number increased to 30,499 in 2000 (Cao, 2004: Table 1). Research impact at the international level has become one of the criteria for institutions to evaluate the achievements of their scholars and for journals to assess their rankings.

Journals in English, the common language in the international research community, have been issued regularly to attract overseas readers as well as contributors. Previously it was a normal practice for articles in most journals to be attached with an English abstract. This has proven to be ineffective because non-Chinese readers are still not able to read the full text even if journals in Chinese can be accessed abroad, which is usually not the case. Journals in English, on the other hand, will possibly receive international subscriptions to bring in profits and status. At this moment in time, English publishing is just beginning and is mainly executed by top-rankcd journals or publishing houses, joint ventures between a Chinese publisher and a foreign business, or foreign publishers that have recently invested in China. There are more than 100 scholarly journals in English published in China, but very few are real world-class journals.

Foreign businesses became interested in China's publishing as early as the 1990s. One of the earliest foreign investments was Bertelsmann, which entered the market by establishing its 'cultural industry company', and later a book club, in Shanghai in 1995. Most of the earliest overseas investors operated their businesses by maintaining a Chinese partner. Some of them, such as Elsevier, are optimistic about business development in China and are seeking independent management. More and more foreign businesses have come to China in the new millennium.

Publication distribution

Shortly after China joined the WTO, the government announced two important policies aiming to open the book distribution market officially to private and foreign ventures. These new policies have inspired and regulated a complete privatization of book wholesaling and retailing. Foreign companies can now set foot not only in book publishing but also in publication distribution. Most major booksellers, such as Amazon.com, are now found in China's market. Private enterprises are becoming involved on a scale larger than before, and some are incorporated. Many private bookstores, also called cultural houses or bookstore cities, have constructed beautiful and spacious buildings with plentiful books and journals. Their active participation in the business has forced the state-run Xinhua Bookstore to undergo a major reform and become a joint stock entity.

Private capital comes to the publication distribution industry from different sources. The major source is privately generated investment funds, followed by joint ownership between collective and private property investments, as well as capital from sources outside the distribution industry. Most of these investments go to retailing enterprises such as bookstores and bookstands, while some capital is directed to wholesaling ventures and chain stores. At the same time, internet bookstores have been rapidly developed and are becoming more popular as an important channel of distributing books.

However, although private investments have created a larger number of bookstores than those owned by the government, state-owned bookstores, because of their size, still handle over 90 per cent of the publication unit sales in the market and have a large percentage of the revenue values. What reforms have brought to these state-owned bookstores is a restructuring of their business by assembling resources to make shareholding enterprises. At the national level a few such incorporated groups are in operation; and many regional distributing groups have been created since 2000. With government support, these groups are able to found large-scale wholesaling and retailing centers to speed up publication distribution.

In order to oversee the development of an open and vigorous publication distribution market, the Books and Periodicals Distribution Association of China was recently established. The association has influenced the development through its nearly 4,000 members from private and state-owned publishers. It has successfully taken over major functions traditionally handled by government agencies, and made efforts to keep the process of publication distribution healthy.

The discussion of book distribution would be incomplete without mentioning various types of book fairs, among which the most famous is the Beijing International Book Fair (BIBF). Initiated in 1986 by the China National Publications Import & Export (Group) Corporation, this international book fair has become the platform through which foreign publications can enter China's book market and foreign publishers can trade books with their Chinese counterparts. Thousands of publishing houses, book salespeople and academic institutions from hundreds of countries, regions and international organizations have participated in the biannual fair. It now has sponsorship from many government agencies, including the State Council's Information Office, the Press and Publications Administration, the State Science and Technology Commission, the Ministries of Culture and Education, Beijing Municipal Government, the Publishers Association of China and the National Copyright Administration, and has become an indispensable arena for the Asian book business. At its twelfth fair in 2005, around 1,500 publishers from 48 countries, regions and organizations participated in the BIBF, with a total of 120,000 titles exhibited and copyright transactions for over 9,000 titles (see www.bibf.net/bibf/bibf/index.jsp).

Digital efforts

Digital communication has been built to international standards since the very beginning of the digital efforts, but did not reach prosperity until the new millennium when ICT matured. The internationalization movement is embraced by libraries through their work on digitizing selected collections. Educational, cultural and research organizations as well as private companies also join the enterprise. With a rapid increase in internet use in China, the accessibility and utilization of online digital materials have increased exponentially both in the general domain and in the academic regime. According to the latest statistics of the China Internet Network Information Center, more than 20 per cent of internet use is for educational purposes. Furthermore, more than 42 per cent of use is for information searches, and 3.9 per cent is for electronic journals (China Internet Network Information Center, 2007).

Over the past six years the development of digital projects has been diverse, reflected by not only varied types of digital content but also varied types of services and management styles. With regard to service types, there are digital content providers such as Tsinghua Tongfang, SSReader, Wanfang Data and VIP Information; electronic publication agents such as Founder and Shusheng; digital content producers and system integrators such as Digital Innovation Technology, Chinasoft and Founder Technology; system integrators for search engines such as TRS, Bai Du and Tell You Information Technology; and system integrators such as Lenovo, Taiji and Huadi. As far as content types are concerned, the current digital environment features those that previously existed, such as electronic books and journals, and those that have newly emerged, such as open access e-print repositories.

In regard to management styles, there are three major types of digital projects – private investment, government sponsorship and academic involvement. Private electronic publishers provide most electronic resources at the present time. In order to compete better in the market, private companies have developed implementation plans to digitize and publish e-materials systematically. Scholarly literature is among the most popular resources supplied. Among private publishers, Fangzheng, SuperStar, Shusheng and Tongfang are best known for their large business size and diverse services. Government initiatives are distinctive in their wide sharing of resources, and expand steadily due to increasing allocations by the government. Major government initiatives include the National Science & Technology Library and the Beijing Academic Library and Information Center. Similarly, individual academic institutions have started their own digital projects and are known for the uniqueness of their e-collections. The latter two provide open access to their online materials to varied degrees.

E-book digitization and publishing are the mainstream in digital projects of all types. Private publishers have a preference for items that may have a broad spectrum of readers, which can be translated into good profits. The majority of e-books produced by SuperStar, for example, are popular items, although no statistics give a detailed breakdown of its over 1 million digitized books. State-sponsored projects concentrate on scholarly literature or materials of historical and cultural value. Taking two statewide educational digital programs as examples, the ongoing Chinese Academic Libraries & Information System (CALIS) project and the China-American Digital Academic Library (CADAL) have each digitized 1 million scholarly items covering Chinese rare books, current books and books in foreign languages, particularly English. CALIS also contracts Fangzheng to set up online databases for college textbooks and associated materials, with a content of more than 20,000 current textbooks and 40,000 textbook references. In total, as many as 1,050 volumes of e-books were digitized and published in 2005, nearly 1,000 times more than the number five years ago (see www.calis.edu.cn/calisnew).

Dissertations and theses are converted into digital formats by different methods. Both state-supported and private-invested digital programs scan them into online databases. Many public and academic libraries also have their own digital plans to digitize theses and dissertations, e.g. the NLC had finished the digitization of 80,000 dissertations by 2005. At the same time, under the CALIS plan, more than 80 academic institutions have recently signed an agreement with a state-operated degree thesis center to contribute to its central database with the metadata elements of their own dissertations and theses in the form of METS and the first 16 pages of each work. A total of 250,000 items are expected to enter this database.

Electronic journals are among the highest priorities in the development of online preservation and dissemination. Each year hundreds of new e-journals and e-newspapers are added to the internet. By 2003 two-thirds of the existing scholarly journals had been digitized, with a total number of more than 12,000. Some private-owned information companies such as Tongfang and Chongqing Weipu are active in providing e-journal databases, and make money from the subscriptions. At Tongfang, the digitization can bring in 2,000 full-text journal articles each day. In addition to Chinese journals, CALIS, supported financially by the government, purchases English e-journal databases from overseas vendors. More than 30,000 scholarly journals are available through its website (www.calis.edu.cn/calisnew). Search functions of e-journals have also been enhanced to support data retrieval by keyword, title and author search, particularly on private-owned and English e-journal databases. Nonetheless, at this moment the functions of searching Chinese journals still have room for improvement, in that only searches by Chinese characters, not Pinyin scripts, are supported.

China began experimenting with open access initiatives in 2003. The earliest efforts were wide-ranging, covering many academic disciplines and not limited to any individual research organization. Three scientific digital repositories, Qiji, Chinese Preprint System and Sciencepaper Online, have been created since 2003 and are still the only comprehensive open access projects today, although several institutional-based repositories have recently appeared. In general, such experiments are quite new to China's scholarly community and have not received much attention from researchers, who are unimpressed by the low quantity and quality of the content items. Their sustainability remains questionable.

Cooperation continues to play an important role in the development of digital projects, including inter-institutional and public-to-private initiatives. Consortium-like practices allow project participants to plan and work together: each party performs different functions and contributes varied resources in digital material creation, description, organization and retrieval. One of the most recent digital projects is the website of Digital Beijing (www.digitalbeijing.gov.cn), which represents the efforts of many organizations to form a comprehensive information service system to cover many aspects of the city of Beijing. It is part of the construction of Digital Olympics for the forthcoming Olympic Games in Beijing in the summer of 2008. Many libraries have contributed to this digital endeavor.

Since the 1990s the digital movement has changed the method of reading publications. More and more people in China now read books online, and there is a continual decrease in numbers reading print materials. The digital movement has also changed the landscape of scholarly communication. Its impact on system infrastructure is noticeable in the way that technology is standardized, management style is reprogrammed and financial support is redistributed. Inside a library where digital projects are initiated, the organizational structure has to be reformed to assign special duties to a designated group of people. The movement's impact on the attitude of scholars is mirrored by their increasing reliance on online resources to conduct research, particularly in science and engineering. In 2006 the circulations of electronic collections in academic libraries were more than ten times higher than in 2003. Such a change is, of course, not unique to China and is a global phenomenon.

Libraries

Libraries have expanded in areas beyond digitization. Taking size as an example, today China has nearly 3,000 public libraries at or above the county level with total collections of around 480 million volumes, and nearly 1,500 academic libraries with total collections of almost 1 billion items. Both school and corporate libraries number approximately 600,000. Specialized libraries have seen the fastest increase in the numbers of libraries and collections: close to 10,000 libraries and more than 1 billion items (National Bureau of Statistics of China, 2007; Library Society of China, 2006).

Most libraries, both regular and digital, in addition to their increase in building size and collections, have expanded service areas and developed tremendous research projects. Library administrators have realized the importance of providing consultation in information seeking and pay more attention to the career development of their librarians. They value professional training of librarians and encourage them to participate actively in scholarly activities, including international exchanges. This is crucial to the efforts of internationalization.

The academic community

Universities are the primary places where scholarly activities have been carried out and research results produced. Both faculty and students have been active in research pursuits. Publication quality and quantity are important components of job evaluation for faculty, and of employment hunting for students if academic jobs are their target. This practice is much like that of the West.

The structure of faculty ranking in China has existed for many decades, and includes professors, associate professors and lecturers – the latter being the equivalent of assistant professors in US universities. Recently, more levels were added to the ladder. One is the title of 'academician', which is awarded by the central government to a professor based on extraordinary contributions and reputation in an academic discipline. In addition to great personal honor and monetary reward, academicians are granted both power to control the promotion of other faculty members in their institution and authority to oversee the distribution of government funding for research nationwide, thus playing a critical role in piloting the development of academia.

Another addition is the title of Changjiang (Yangtze) scholar, introduced by the government's 'Changjiang Scholar and Development Plan of Innovation Team' initiative in 1998, with the purpose of bringing internationally known scholars to higher educational institutions. Unlike an academician, whose title is permanent, a Changjiang scholar has a tenure of three years, during which he/she enjoys a much higher salary than a regular professor and has a fixed research grant of 2 million yuan in natural sciences or half a million in the humanities and social sciences. Changjiang scholars are divided into special professors and visiting professors. A special professor works full time for at least nine months a year for the host university, while a visiting professor is asked to work full time for at least three months (two months by exception). Because of the selection criterion of 'internationally known', most Changjiang scholars are those who received a degree from an overseas university or whose primary work is in a foreign research institution. The number of Changjiang scholars and academicians at a university is limited, and only top-ranked universities can afford to accommodate them.

Furthermore, regular professors have different statuses designed to distinguish them from each other. In most cases, lecturers are not eligible to supervise graduate students, and associate professors can have masters students but cannot supervise doctoral students. A full professor may only supervise masters students if entitled 'master's advisor' by the State Education Commission, or may have the authority to supervise both masters and doctoral students if entitled 'doctoral advisor'. Although a doctoral advisor is superior to a master's advisor, they are at the same rank of professor. The number of doctoral advisors is a symbol of prestige for a university – the more the better. In many universities undergraduate education is the work of professors whose rank is lower than doctoral advisor and thus whose age is younger in general. Junior faculty take full responsibility for teaching undergraduate classes, and at the same time carry out extensive research activities for their career development.

In addition to higher educational institutions, another academic system, namely the Chinese academies, is a major part of the academic community. The system started in 1928 when the Academia Sinica was founded to support research activities in sciences, humanities and social sciences. Although the Academia Sinica was moved to Taiwan after the Communist Party took over the mainland, it was immediately replaced by the Chinese Academy of Sciences (CAS), run under the State Council of China. In 1977 the Chinese Academy of Social Sciences (CASS), also reporting to the State Council, was established out of the CAS to work exclusively on social sciences and the humanities. In 1994 the Chinese Academy of Engineering was created to boost the development of engineering and technology. The former two have regional branches and offices in some provinces as well as their main headquarters in Beijing. At the same time, all provinces and municipalities have replicated the CAS and CASS to establish their own academies of sciences and social sciences.

These academies at different levels have accommodated thousands of full-time researchers all over the country, making the system a giant in the academic community. Taking the CAS as an example, it has five sections – mathematics, physics, chemistry, technology and earth sciences – covering more than 100 institutes, one university, one graduate school, four documentation and information centers, two news and publishing units and hundreds of science- and technology-based enterprises. Similarly, the CASS is structured into 31 institutes and over 50 centers with approximately 3,000 researcher employees at senior, intermediate and junior levels. Unlike university professors, scholars at the CAS and CASS and their provincial replicates do not have responsibility for teaching and are assigned to undertake research activities only. They have thus contributed much to the scholarly community in ways such as publishing research journals, many top-ranked, and managing professional associations, many at the national level.

In addition to the academies, the so-called *shi ye dan wei* (cultural institutions), such as museums and public libraries, also employ full-time scholars to carry out research projects. These *shi ye dan wei* are run by government agencies and have recently suffered from an increasing shortage of funding under the reforms. Unlike other modernization programs, most *shi ye dan wei* are still struggling today for necessary research support and even for their own survival. An example is that many museums relinquish exhibition space to allow commercial vending in return for necessary capital.

In order to promote scientific research, the government has established several national foundations to manage funds for scientists and social scientists. The National Natural Science Foundation of China (NSFC) is one, and supports innovative research projects. According to the NSFC, it has funded more than 52,000 scientific projects in varied categories with a total sum of 6.6 billion yuan (see www.nsfc.gov.cn/e_nsfc/2006/04pa/index.htm and www.nsfc.gov.cn/e_nsfc/2006/01au/11a.htm). Over 85 per cent of the articles published in *Nature* and *Science* by Chinese scholars in the past few years received sponsorship from the NSFC. Unfortunately, government foundations are the only financial resources that scholars can possibly depend on for their scientific research; and only a small portion of scientific projects can benefit from their assistance.

It is very rare that professional associations are independent in nature, although some may claim to be so. Instead, they are mostly managed and sponsored by research institutions or government agencies either directly or indirectly. As in other countries, these associations function by organizing conferences, publishing journals and circulating research data and results. Because of different supporting resources, financially and intellectually, national-level academic societies provide a higher quality of services than local and regional societies, though exceptions exist. Most national research societies maintain a large membership and hold influential conferences, playing an active role in the circulation of scholarly information.

Copyright

Copyright is a sensitive issue in the discussion of scholarly communication, given that Western countries have complained about China's inadequate work on stopping piracy in publishing and international trade. However, it is a complex issue because the making and implementation of copyright law are closely related to the conditions of a country, including its politics, economy and culture, since the notion of 'property' is a cultural norm. Having adopted its first copyright law in 1991 and joined the Berne Convention for the Protection of Literary and Artistic Works in 1992, China has only a short history of making and enforcing copyright law and needs time to perfect the system.

Technically, the Chinese copyright law largely meets the requirements of the Universal Copyright Convention. The formation of China's law was influenced by many international copyright treaties, including the Berne Convention, the Agreement on Trade Related Aspects of Intellectual Property Rights (TRIPS) and the WIPO Copyright and Performances and Phonographs Treaties. Of course, there may still be certain shortfalls, such as China's incomplete stipulations over public performances and broadcasting rights. Major problems also lie in network copyright protection as the result of a rapid development of ICT in the country. However, the efforts to build a digital rights management system are universal, although China has its own unique situation.

Criticism of China's copyright focuses primarily on how intellectual property rights have been enforced in practice and what consequences have arisen. As mentioned above, copyright is relatively new to China. For almost a century both the Nationalist and Communist Parties ignored the importance of protecting intellectual property. It was not until the early 1980s, when Deng Xiaoping advocated 'legalization', that the need to reconstruct the legal system to work against piracy and counterfeiting of intellectual property was emphasized. Thus ordinary Chinese people lack the necessary historical roots in understanding copyright and do not usually take it seriously. When people have no respect for copyright and are under pressure to achieve success economically, breaches of copyright law are inevitable. Appropriate punishment is the right action for such violations and can function to educate people on its importance. Such education has failed to some degree, because for many years the punishments were either too rare or too minor to alert citizens to the seriousness of the crime. The government has been looking to balance copyright protection and economic development; and China's complex network of bureaucracies may make actual enforcement inefficient.

In any sense, a government can play an influential role in creating a culture that respects property. In reality, the Chinese government did make great efforts to crack down on piracy and counterfeiting, particularly after China acceded to the WTO and TRIPS in 2001. Whether the efforts represent bowing to external pressure or are the result of internal reforms, the fact remains that pirates now find it harder to violate copyright law.

The practice of copyright protection in scholarly conduct is more complicated because violations may take varied forms and are difficult to detect, and also because some violations may have only caused ethical dilemmas and are legally innocent. Early in this chapter the existence of plagiarism and cheating in scholarly publications was discussed. In recent years several scholars decided to fight against this misbehavior by taking personal action to protect academia. For example, Fang Zhou Zi, He Zuo Ma and Si Ma Nan, all famous scholars, have devoted their time to collecting information about scholars' misbehavior in research. They set up websites, like New Threads (www.xys.org), to collect evidence, and established private foundations, such as the Organization for Scientific & Academic Integrity in China, to give financial support to people fighting against copyright violations in the scholarly community. It is valuable that personal efforts are made to combat academic dishonesty; yet it is more important that a strong system of academic evaluations is created to safeguard scientific integrity in a structured way.

Piracy does exist in scholarly publishing in the reproduction of books and, particularly, audiovisual material. Libraries are cautious about illegal publications in their acquisitions. In general, such publications fall into three categories: those with illegal content, like inciting subversion of government authority and propagandizing feudal superstitions; those created by illegal industry qualifications; and those that infringe on the copyrights of others. The last category is the major source of pirated publications and deserves careful verification. Among various strategies of authentication in practice, selection of top-quality suppliers and inclusion of a copyright clause in every license agreement or purchase contract are the most important ones to guarantee copyright.

Since the mid-1990s computer networks have created new challenges for owners of copyright-protected works and have presented additional ways to exploit them. Academically, copyright control for electronic journals and databases, or the lack of it, is an example of such new digital challenges. At the beginning of the digitization process, Chinese e-projects tended to deal with copyright issues only when they encountered problems; and unauthorized texts might have been included in some e-databases. According to China's copyright law, publishers possess the copyright for journals and authors own the copyright for individual articles. This posed difficulties for digital creators in contacting individual authors for permission for the online publication of their articles, leaving potential disputes between authors and electronic publishers. Although many e-projects have worked hard to obtain copyright from authors, publishers and other copyright-collecting agencies, precaution is by no means unnecessary. Most recently, publishers began asking authors to sign over their copyrights to the publishers for both print and electronic versions of their articles. It is obvious that China's copyright law will need to be regularly revised to meet the ever-changing situation as information technology develops, and to be more compliant with international conventions.

Conclusion

This chapter has attempted to draw a picture of the development of scholarly communication in China throughout history. Emphasis has been put on the discussion of achievements, as well as issues raised at each stage of this development and solutions to those problems. The path of scholarly communication to modernization and internationalization has never been straightforward, always being a part of concurrent political and economic pursuits. However, this chapter only covers a small part of the entire scholarly communication story. Only those parts that are both unique and traditional to this country have been described. It is certain that modern China has achieved amazing accomplishments in economic growth and technological advancement that have helped shape a colorful and increasingly healthy scholarly communication system, contributing a great deal to the diversity of the world.

2

Scholarly communication in Hong Kong and Macao

Steven K. Luk

Located in the southernmost Chinese mainland, Hong Kong and Macao are two Special Administrative Regions (SARs) of the People's Republic of China. Before their handover to China in the late 1990s, both were European colonies. Their colonial history could be traced back to the Opium War after Great Britain defeated China around 1840. China was forced to cede the rights of Hong Kong and Macao to the UK and Portugal, and permitted their permanent occupation and the establishment of governments in these areas. Under the control of the Europeans for more than a hundred years, both Hong Kong and Macao developed a capitalist economy and democratic politics, and were famous as an international financial center and a gambling/tourist hub respectively.

The transfers of their sovereignty to China took place in 1997 (Hong Kong) and 1999 (Macao). Thereafter, their relationship to mainland China has been maintained under the principle of 'one country, two systems', in which they are able to enjoy a high degree of autonomy except in defense and foreign affairs, which are controlled by the central Chinese government. Their own legal and financial systems, customs and immigration policies and delegations to international organizations remain virtually unchanged. Their scholarly communication system is pretty much the same as before.

However, changes in scholarly conduct are unavoidable when economic interdependency and cultural interactions become more and more intensive and dynamic between Hong Kong and Macao and the mainland. The following sections give evidence of these interactions in almost every aspect of scholarly activities, such as in educational development, publishing pursuits and the like.

Educational system in Hong Kong

Based on sheer numbers, higher education has been a flourishing business in both Hong Kong and Macao. The number of tertiary institutions in Hong Kong that enjoy the prestigious title of 'university' has increased to eight, from only two 15 years ago. Also, one would have hesitated to include Macao in this discussion were it not for the Macao government's conscientious promotion of and increased funding for higher education in the last few years, partly owing to revenues earned from the entertainment business. The Macao SAR is now also promoting higher education and scholarship.

Education in Hong Kong, especially higher education, is still a government business as the government provides almost 90 per cent of the entire budget. Although actual allocation is done through a public body called the University Grants Committee, its members are appointed by the government, and a large number of university council members are appointed by the chief executive, the nominal chancellor of the universities, by the Legislative Council, the political structure of which the government controls overwhelmingly, and by very conservative public bodies. This formula is uniformly applied to all seven of the public universities.

In summer 2007 a series of hearings was held to investigate the secretary of the Hong Kong Education Bureau with regard to his intervention in the academic freedom of the Hong Kong Institute of Education (HKIED, which has been lobbying for university status) and the government's efforts to force a merger among institutions in higher education. Quite recently Shue Yan College was bestowed the title of a private 'university', having engaged in higher education for over four decades. Also, the university system will be changing to a four-year degree in line with universities in this region, rather than the three-year degree favored by the British. These are all recent developments in the higher education field.

A heavy reliance on government funding has it benefits: all administrative and teaching staff used to enjoy security, excellent salaries and sundry fringe benefits, all linked to those of the civil service. They did not have to be creative and entrepreneurial, as salaries were guaranteed and promotion was based on seniority. This system has been challenged in recent years owing to government budget deficits in the face of the Asian financial crisis in 1998, the advent of technology and globalism as more local students can afford a higher education overseas, and, to a certain extent, the more entrepreneurial if not profit-making approach of universities on the Chinese mainland.

Indeed, the government has been giving more autonomy to university educators in recent years, although this may not guarantee the best results as university administrators who came up through the seniority system have neither the vision nor the courage to bring about change. It has been reported that scholarly output, in terms of publications, has been greatly enhanced owing to funding competition (University Grants Committee, 1999, 2006). Nevertheless, a good deal of money is spent in public and media relations as all seven universities complete for media coverage. Airport advertising and seminars at five-star hotels are common vehicles adopted by local universities for promotion. Professional and business disciplines are attracting more attention and funding at the expense of the arts and sciences. Will academic freedom be sacrificed in the face of funding squeezes and bureaucratic intervention? In 2003 the vice chancellor of the University of Hong Kong, Professor Y.C. Cheng, resigned after his administrative intervention into the polling on the issue of popular support for the chief executive conducted by junior faculty in the Department of Sociology. As mentioned above, a series of hearings has been conducted on the secretary of the Department of Education and Manpower, Dr Arthur Li, on his intervention into the academic freedom of the teaching staff in the Hong Kong Institute of Education. To what extent will academic quality be compromised in the quest for an increased number of college graduates? How will overseas-educated PhDs help to promote local scholarship and research in the long run? And is the ruling élite (senior bureaucrats and business tycoons) satisfied with the universities' contribution to the local economy? These questions will remain unanswered for some time to come.

The scholarly tradition: East and West

China has long based its traditional scholarship on the system by which successive dynasties staffed its imperial bureaucracy. Education, mainly reading, writing and calligraphy, was provided by individual families or large clans in the village at an early age, because imperial success would enhance the prestige and possibly wealth and power of the village clans as both the judiciary and administrative functions of the locality were in the hands of the magistrate. The child was nurtured in Confucian doctrines so that he could construct an ideal social order when he grew up. Thus traditional scholarship included 'Confucian discourse (*cizhang*), poetry (*shi*) and philology (*kaoju*)', which is different from the concept of scholarship in the West. The dispute as to the definition of scholarship still plagues academia in Hong Kong, where East meets West and faculty members are as diverse in origin as in social background. This especially bothers faculty members who are locally educated, some of whom do not have a doctoral degree.

Another frequent area of dispute during the appraisal exercise is the medium in which a piece was written and the location where it was published. Publications in the English language, particularly by university presses, are more professionally edited and refereed, whereas Chinese publications are seldom refereed, if at all, except those published by the university presses in Hong Kong and a few publishers in Taiwan, notably publications from the Academia Sinica. Should academic publication in Chinese be treated *pari passu* with that in English in terms of tenure consideration? Also, since the quality of manuscripts is so uneven, should non-refereed publication be regarded as academic publication in considering promotion and advancement? Scholarship in the West prizes originality and source citation above all; this format does not always appear in traditional Chinese scholarly works.

It is well known that only publications put out by university presses (thus probably peer reviewed) are acknowledged as academic publications in terms of advancement in academia. The problem is that Hong Kong academicians are increasingly publishing their works in mainland China, allegedly for a wider readership and/or greater publicity. It is common knowledge that many mainland Chinese publishing houses, including eminent university publishers, will publish manuscripts for a cash subsidy, not to mention the lack of any peer-review process. Also, as more and more academic exchanges are carried out across the border, the kind of *guanxi* thus cultivated runs beyond relations between a publisher and its authors. The trend is that more and more works by Hong Kong scholars are published in Chinese in the mainland, particularly in the social sciences and the humanities where they are more acceptable. Additionally, the cost is lower should the author need to pay for publication.

Why should a scholarly work be published in Hong Kong or elsewhere but not in China, whether in Chinese or English? The writer can think of the following justifications.

- It is a bilingual work, and probably Hong Kong has the best bilingual editorial staff compared to any place in the world. In fact, both Taiwanese and mainland Chinese academic publishers admire Hong Kong's ability to produce bilingual works and thus have a voice in both English- and Chinese-speaking worlds.

- It is about Hong Kong and South China.

- It is in Chinese and the contents are so sensitive in nature that they cannot be truthfully published in the mainland. This includes topics on contemporary history, and recollections and memoirs of eminent figures. Mainland authors are sometimes encouraged to have these types of manuscripts published in Hong Kong, where there is still academic freedom of expression.

- It is a textbook or training materials for local use, as Hong Kong has a very vibrant market for teaching materials. Both Pearson and the Oxford University Press maintain a sizeable presence in Hong Kong to publish school textbooks. The total numbers of their employees amount to 420 and 350 respectively.

Academic institutions and their publishers in Hong Kong

Academic publishing loosely defined includes the following categories of scholarly publications.

- Those published by the university presses: these manuscripts are usually refereed and often co-published with overseas publishing houses in order to break out of the territorial confinement.

- Those published by university-affiliated research institutes: many of these are monographs on specific topics; some are topical pamphlets related to local research on politics and social, educational and health issues. They are also more policy-oriented, thus they need to come out on a timely basis.

- Ceremonial types of publications: the quality varies in this area, with examples ranging from real scholarly papers on a Ming history project to papers from ceremonial conferences funded by the SAR government to celebrate the tenth anniversary of Hong Kong's handover back to China. Many government agencies under the Arts Development Council, for instance, administer archives and research projects.

- Publications on topics of local interest. Examples are the Hong Kong Film Archives and the Hong Kong Government Archives, which are engaged in publication of their related research and holdings. Government departments and public bodies/companies have also published books to commemorate their anniversaries because they want their contribution to be known and their voice heard in society. These beautifully designed pictorials can also be used as souvenirs when visiting their counterparts in the mainland.

Other than academic titles published by the four university presses, it is not easy to acquire the sundry publications put out by various bodies. Firstly, the sponsor institution may not be a scholarly body; thus the publication of these titles is open to tender. They may be produced but not 'published'. Secondly, the publisher which won the job may be relatively unknown and put out very few publications. Thirdly, they lack recognition and distribution and sales capabilities; thus acquisition is difficult even locally, not to mention by overseas libraries. Fortunately, two university presses, namely the Chinese University Press and the Hong Kong University Press, have recently entered into distribution relationships with many of the minor presses and individuals, so their titles can be purchased overseas from their respective websites. Major academic publishing houses are listed below.

The University of Hong Kong Press

Founded in 1964, this is the oldest academic publisher in the territory. It is a department of the University of Hong Kong, the oldest of Hong Kong's eight universities, established in 1902 to provide appropriate education to young men who wanted to pursue a civil service career in the colonial administration. It used to be closely tied to the 'British imperial order'.

The Hong Kong University Press used to reflect the values and interests of the institution to which it is related. It once published many textbooks for the university's entrance examination. Its director was a retiree of a major British publishing house in Hong Kong, probably through connection rather than by design; many of its titles were accounts of British imperial activities in Hong Kong and elsewhere in Asia/Africa.

The press now publishes around 45 titles annually on average, most of which are in English. Some of the titles are Asian paperback editions of hardback originals issued by major universities in the USA. The purpose is to make these works affordable and more easily accessible to readers in Hong Kong and Asia.

The Hong Kong University Press has been assiduously trying to develop closer relations with the US market, and has successfully developed manuscripts in Hong Kong studies, film and cultural studies. It also publishes monographs put out by the Hong Kong chapter of the Royal Asiatic Society (again an 'imperial' connection) and the university's Faculty of Education. The press has an agreement with the University of Washington Press in Seattle to distribute its titles in North America.

The Chinese University Press

Established in 1964, the Chinese University of Hong Kong is a bilingual institution purposely set up to educate the offspring of the refugees who flooded Hong Kong when the communists took over the mainland in the late 1940s. The population of Hong Kong increased from half a million at the end of the Second World War to 2.5 million a decade later. Education, housing and medical services had to be provided in this growing city, which within another decade turned into one of the four little 'dragons'.

Prior to the opening of mainland China in 1979, and the lifting of censorship in Taiwan in the mid-1980s, Hong Kong was the only Chinese territory that enjoyed freedom of speech and expression, and the Chinese University of Hong Kong was the home of many overseas Chinese/Taiwanese scholars who traveled to Asia visiting relatives or conducting research during their sabbatical leaves. The Chinese University Press was the publisher of their works in Chinese. Important authors included P.T. Ho, Yao Tsung-I, D.C. Lau, Li Tien-yi, Cheng Te-k'wan and Stuart R. Schram.

Today China scholars in the USA of Chinese ancestry increasingly come from the mainland, and conducting research in the social sciences with mainland institutions is relatively uninhibited. The Chinese University Press has turned its attention more to the study of China by local scholars. Recent statistics show that two-thirds of its authors are local and one-third from overseas (the USA, Australia and the UK). About 62 per cent of its publications are sold locally, 18 per cent go to Taiwan and 16 per cent to North America; the rest are sold in Japan, the Chinese mainland, the UK, etc. Two-thirds of its publications are in Chinese, thus it is a truly bilingual publisher.

The Chinese University Press is an overseas member of the Association of American University Presses (AAUP). Its English titles are distributed worldwide by Columbia University Press, and all titles are sold through Sino-United Logistics in Taiwan.

There are two categories of publications: academic books and general/textbooks. Most academic books are in English, and all need to go through the peer-review and committee process. The Chinese University Press has focused on developing several lines of publications:

- scholarly manuscripts in the humanities and sciences in the China/Hong Kong field;
- memoirs and recollections of the Cultural Revolution, as many of these manuscripts are still not publishable inside the mainland;
- a bilingual series on modern Chinese literature;
- Chinese learning texts and materials for English native speakers;
- academic journals.

The City University Press

Founded in 1997, this is the youngest of the three local university presses. Being limited in resources, it publishes fewer than 20 titles annually, mostly manuscripts from its own faculty. It also publishes textbooks/reference books for some of the university's writing and management programs.

The press is used mainly as a vehicle of the university for advertising and promotion purposes. Nevertheless, it is a demonstration of the university's commitment to Chinese and humanistic studies, as advocated by its former president, Professor Chang Hsin-kong.

The Oxford University Press (China)

Founded in the early 1970s, this is one of the oldest educational publishers in Hong Kong. With Pearson Longman, it probably shares more than half of the lucrative textbook market from kindergarten to high school. The author was told some time ago by the press's senior management that it has been OUP's most lucrative subsidiary. OUP-China covers sales in Hong Kong, China (through sublicensing agreements) and Macao. Its major revenues come from textbook publishing – ELT (English language teaching) materials, bilingual dictionaries and local textbooks in both English and Chinese.

OUP-China ventured into academic publishing in the early 1990s, when it embarked on a series of translations from English into Chinese of social sciences titles about China/Asia and also published semi-academic titles on topics in Hong Kong studies. This type of publishing was discontinued in the late 1990s, probably because it could not meet the company's guidelines on investment return.

In lieu of academic titles, OUP-China now publishes some trade-oriented titles, which fall into two categories. The first, by far the more lucrative, is sensational memoirs and recollections written by mainland authors. The second category is light manuscripts/short pieces on culture, arts and customs written by well-known public intellectuals in Hong Kong. Many of the pieces have previously appeared in newspapers and magazines.

It is known that decisions on Chinese-language titles can be made locally, and need not be refereed by outside bodies nor reviewed by the editorial authorities in London. The brand OUP can attract attention and readership. The present writer does not know whether these works are regarded as academic publications by Hong Kong universities for advancement purposes. It is thus a pity that, for a premier name such as OUP, its commitment in Hong Kong does not go beyond making money.

Scholarly publications in Macao

Before the handover in 1999, Macao had very little academic activity, let alone publishing. Its population was a mere 400,000, and the number of casino gambling (entertainment) employees was second only to that of government employees. It lacked both physical and financial infrastructures; thus it also lacked the vibrant middle class on which Hong Kong's economy depends. The University of East Asia, the only institution to offer higher education, changed its name from Macao University. Even high school textbooks were older editions previously used in Hong Kong because the students could not afford new ones.

This situation has changed since the handover. Macao's link with the mainland has proved essential, as it offers unique entertainment that the mainland Chinese cannot find within their borders. Secondly, the SAR government has introduced competition into the casino business. Thirdly, the stationing of the PLA (People's Liberation Army) has proven to be essential to public safety. The efforts to preserve Macao's heritage and urban renovation have drawn in visitors and tourists in addition to gambling clients. Recent statistics reveal that Macao's per capita GDP has rivaled that of Hong Kong: the monthly median income of the employed was 5,167 patacas in 2004, 5,773 in 2005 and 6,701 in 2006 (Macau SAR Government, 2007). A technical college has been set up in addition to the university.

Aware of its image and handicaps, the government has put in substantial resources to boost its international standing through investments in education and culture. Thus publishing has been thriving in recent years. According to Macao Central Library figures, the number of publications (via ISBN counts) increased from 199 in 2000 to 377 in 2006 (Instituto Cultural do Governo da R.A.E. de Macau, 2007). Obviously, the bulk of publications were yearbooks, manuals and reference books on Macao. Nevertheless, these are precisely the types of publications useful to overseas research libraries.

The most notable semi-academic publisher is the Publication Center of the Universidade de Macau, which was established in 1995. It publishes research findings, conference proceedings and scholarly monographs. There are more than 100 titles in Chinese, Portuguese and English in print over a wide variety of disciplines in the arts and languages, social sciences, natural sciences and technology. It also publishes textbooks which are unique to the university's courses.

To the extent that the government is generously hiring staff from overseas and funding academic conferences and seminars on the study of Macao, one can expect publishing activities to continue. Conference organizers have also recently been encouraged to publish their research findings with Hong Kong/overseas academic publishers on a subvention basis to widen their influence. One of the active funding sources is the Fundacao Macau, which has played a major role in funding publications on Macao's history, heritage, arts and letters.

As fledging academic institutions, the overall quality of the publications put out by these institutions is still uneven. Nevertheless, for scholars whose specialty is Macao or overseas Portuguese activities these publications would constitute a goldmine, as many are original records in Portuguese. Current scholarship is more focused on the political, social, cultural and economic integration of Macao with the hinterland and with Hong Kong. Most of the publications are available via the Chinese University Press, which acts as the overseas distributor.

Publications by research institutes and public archives in Hong Kong

Although perhaps not as noticeable as university presses, research organizations and archives have contributed substantially though not directly to the scholarly publications of Hong Kong. Some are directly related to the universities and faculty departments, while others are semi-government public institutions whose role is to preserve the heritage or to disseminate government information.

It should also be recognized that most of these publications are restricted to the limited functions of the institutions which publish them: precisely because of this, they are invaluable to local research on Hong Kong. Notable institutions which act as publishers are discussed below.

Institutions related to the Chinese University of Hong Kong

Three out of the four foundational colleges of the university have publication units, publishing memoirs and reminiscences, college histories and reprints of speeches and articles written by founding faculty members. Additionally, some departments in the humanities, such as the Department of Chinese Language and Literature, also engage in publishing faculty research findings, although their circulation is much more limited and the publications are only available upon request.

Institute of Chinese Studies

This institute is made up of several entities publishing both scholarly monographs and journals. The former are mostly put out by the Center for Chinese Archaeology and Art and the Research Center for Translation. Several important scholarly magazines have been published here, including *The Twenty-first Century*, *Rendition* and a local dialect research bulletin. High-quality exhibition/collection catalogs come out regularly from the Art Museum and the Center for Chinese Archaeology and Art, which has a research team involved in excavations in Hong Kong/Macao sites and relics under the South China Sea. The Research Center for Chinese Ancient Texts has published numerous volumes on the concordance of ancient Chinese works, all of which are distributed commercially via the Commercial Press (HK) and the Chinese Press. The center was first conceived by Professor D.C. Lau, who has since retired; the work is now carried on by his students, who concurrently teach in the Chinese Department.

Hong Kong Institute of Educational Research

This institute publishes two journals in Chinese on local education and primary education. They serve as important means of communication among teachers and educators. Aside from this, the institute also puts out occasional papers on issues of education in Hong Kong. These are timely pieces oriented towards government policy.

Hong Kong Institute of Asia-Pacific Studies

This institute is perhaps a misnomer. Its focus is mostly on social and economic research related to China and Hong Kong. The more scholarly works have been co-published with the Chinese University Press, while research pamphlets are published in the form of policy-oriented occasional papers. The institute has recently conducted research, including telephone sampling for various clients such as the government of Hong Kong, which has recently awarded the institute many social research projects.

Research institutions related to the University of Hong Kong

Compared with publications put out by the institutes related to the Chinese University, research reports/monographs published by the University of Hong Kong are mostly Hong Kong and Asia related and mostly in English, which is the official medium of instruction of the university. It tries to bring local (Hong Kong and Asian in this case) information to the Western world, whereas the Chinese University of Hong Kong is a bilingual institution which prides itself on promoting cultural exchange and bridging the cultural gap between China and the West. As such, there is much more scholarly exchange with mainland/Taiwanese scholars in the latter institution.

The university's schools and departments are engaged in publishing. A notable case is the School of Chinese, which for some time edited a scholarly journal entitled the *Journal of Oriental Studies*. It was unfortunately discontinued in recent years. The Faculty of Education also publishes monographs and research results under its own imprint.

Center of Asian Studies

This center has long been an active vehicle trying to bring Hong Kong/Asia to Hong Kong's non-Chinese community. It was a forum and a training camp for British diplomats on Chinese studies. The center's focus often varies in accordance with the academic interests of its directors: economic history under Professor Frank H.H. King, the local economy under Professor Edward Chan and now social and cultural issues under Professor Wong Siu Lun, a sociologist by training. The center administers several programs, namely the China-ASEAN Project, the China-India project and a project on local culture and society. It conducts lectures and seminars and produces research findings, some of which are published in the forms of monographs and occasional papers under the center's auspices. The publications are for sale on its own website.

The APEC Center

This center aims to coordinate research efforts in policy issues with regard to the economy of the Asia Pacific region. It is sponsored by the university's Faculty of Business and Economics, with an affiliation to the Hong Kong Center for Economic Research. The center puts out a vast amount of statistics, helps to foster research networks and conducts seminars and workshops. It publishes monographs and occasional papers, plus very up-to-date online information on the region.

Asian Case Research Center

This is a research center affiliated with the Faculty of Business and Economics of the university. Established in 1997, it addresses the growing demand for research and instructional materials on Asian business. It tries to position itself as a repository of business cases in China/Hong Kong and foster ties with the business communities in the region. The cases are available for sale.

Center for the Advancement in Special Education

This center was set up under the auspices of the Faculty of Education. It conducts research and seminars, some of which are published under the center's auspices.

Research institutes related to the City University of Hong Kong

As a newly established city university with a mission to develop community education, the City University of Hong Kong has been trying to push itself into the big league of 'research universities', so to speak, in line with the University of Hong Kong, the Chinese University of Hong Kong and the Hong Kong University of Science and Technology. This was especially the case under one able and ambitious president, Professor Chang Hsin Kang. Indeed, it has successfully established a new media school and developed various kinds of educational programs in lieu of the traditional arts and sciences curricula for higher education. As such, many of the university's research programs are unique in their own fields.

The Chinese Civilization Center is one of the showpieces that Professor Chang created in this newly founded university. It takes over the role of teaching general education in liberal arts colleges, and aims to provide students with knowledge on various elements and aspects of China's cultural achievements. To strengthen students' cultural competence, understanding the Chinese cultural heritage is an essential part of students' intellectual wealth, academic excellence and future careers. Obviously, this 'politically correct' statement won Professor Chang friends and enemies when Hong Kong was going through its transition from a British colony to an SAR under Chinese sovereignty. Nevertheless, the Chinese Civilization Center provides classes and seminars in various aspects of Chinese cultural and performing arts, facilitates exchanges with scholars in the field and publishes works of a more general nature for Hong Kong's reading public.

There are many research centers and programs within the university, notably the Southeast Asia Research Center, the Governance in Asia Research Center and the Center for Chinese and Comparative Law. Most publish newsletters and research results in the form of monographs and occasional papers. An example is the *Hong Kong Journal of Social Sciences* under the stewardship of Professor Joseph Cheng. The shortcoming of this set-up is that most centers lack long-term funding and commitment and depend on the prestige and connections of academicians. Thus the demise of a center usually follows shortly after the departure/retirement of its director.

Other institutions

There are academic and semi-academic publications from research institutes of universities such as the Lingnan University, Polytechnic University and Baptist University, but most are in the form of conference proceedings of uneven quality and irregular circulation. The Hong Kong

University of Science and Technology encourages its staff members to publish only in overseas refereed journals. This is viable, as most of its research fields are in management, economics and natural sciences. Also, as it was founded in the late 1980s, most of its faculty members are American trained and well connected to the international publishing world.

One should also pay attention to the publications of government museums and archives. The Hong Kong Film Archives has produced some excellent studies on the history of local firms. Government bodies and commercial banks and houses also disseminate information regularly on the economy and social welfare data on Hong Kong, which may be of value in academic research.

Academic journals and scholarly magazines in Hong Kong

This area was touched on briefly in previous sections. There are only a few journals of academic renown that originate in Hong Kong, and many of these are in Chinese with very limited circulation. This is a problem of journal publication in general, as the more professional the journal, the more limited its circulation and the less likely it can be published on a business basis by a commercial publisher; and this is exactly the case for a small academic community such as Hong Kong. Nevertheless, there are several long-standing academic journals of some repute. The following are currently either published or distributed by the Chinese University Press, the only academic publisher that has developed a small journal program.

- *Journal of the Institute of Chinese Studies* appears yearly, and is distributed by the Chinese University Press. The institute is part of the Chinese University of Hong Kong. This is a respectable journal on traditional Chinese studies in the humanities, especially history and Chinese literature.

- *The Chinese Review: An Interdisciplinary Journal on Greater China*, published by the Chinese University Press. This is a refereed journal in its sixth year of publication, and is indexed by the Social Science Citation Index among others. It covers issues of academic interest relating to modern and contemporary China.

- *The Twenty-five Century* (*Ershi-i shiji*) is a quarterly in Chinese published by the Institute of Chinese Studies at the Chinese University of Hong Kong. It can trace its origins to the early 1990s when several mainland scholars, alienated by what happened in Beijing subsequent to the Tiananmen student uprising, started publication of this magazine.

- *Ching Feng*, started under the title of *Quarterly Notes* in 1957, is the official organ of the Christian Study Center on Chinese Religion and Culture. Its self-proclaimed purpose is to 'promote critical and innovative investigations into all aspects of the study of Chinese Christianity, Chinese religions, and inter-religious dialogues between Christian and other Asian religions'.

- *Translation Quarterly* is published semi-annually by the Hong Kong Translation Society. Being a bilingual society, translation studies in literature, law and business have been better developed in Hong Kong than in other Chinese cities.

- *Rendition* is one of the longest-lasting magazines, with a focus on the English translation of mainland authors in literature. It is put out by the Center of Translation Research at the Institute of Chinese Studies, Chinese University of Hong Kong.

The following journals have appeared in the past few years under the auspices of learned societies of their respective disciplines in Hong Kong.

- *Asian Journal of English Language Teaching*, under the editorship of Professors Gwendolyn Gong and George S. Braine of the English Department at the Chinese University of Hong Kong.

- *Asian Anthropology*, under the editorship of Professors Tan Chee-Beng and Gordon Mathews, also at the Chinese University of Hong Kong.

- *Journal of Psychology in Chinese Society*, sponsored by the Hong Kong Psychological Society. It is a semi-annual, currently under the editorship of Professor Charles C. Chan of the Chinese University of Hong Kong.

- *Journal of Translation Studies*, sponsored by the Translation Department of the Chinese University of Hong Kong. It is a semi-annual, and faculty members take turns to serve as editors.

- *Journal of Communication and Society* (*Quanbo yu shehui xuekan*) is a bulletin which tries to bridge the gap between practitioners and academics in media studies. It is in Chinese, and deliberately tries to communicate with colleagues in the mainland. It has entered its second year of publication.

- *The Drama Bulletin* (*Xianggang siju xuekan*) appears semi-annually in Chinese. Sponsored by the Drama Works at the Lady Shaw Hall, Chinese University of Hong Kong, it focuses on the studies of local theatrical art.

- *Educational Journal* (*Jiaoyu xuebo*) is a semi-annual for the study of education in Hong Kong. It is published by the Hong Kong Institute of Education Research, affiliated with the Faculty of Education in the Chinese University of Hong Kong.

Over the years some of these journals (such as the *Journal of Lingnan University*, *Quest*, *Journal of Social Sciences* and the *Hong Kong Journal of Society*) have disappeared, owing to a lack of good articles and/or funding, as very few of them can stand financially on their own. Most journals have adopted some sort of referee system, although quality depends on the levels of editorial acumen as well as adequate submission. There is also ambivalence about language, because a journal is likely to attract more articles if it is in Chinese; this then limits its circulation among overseas scholars and libraries. The circulation of academic publications of Hong Kong origin is still limited in the mainland, perhaps because of the contents and perhaps because research in the humanities and social sciences is only marginally important and relatively offensive in China's current pursuit of a strong polity. Given that the academic authorities in Hong Kong claim to accept only articles published by international journals on the basis of academic merit, publishing research results in Chinese implies sub-standard quality and might even be penalized (as it indicates the author lacks ability to publish for an international audience). This may not matter to veteran scholars, but it does hurt junior faculty members in the case of tenure and promotion considerations.

Conclusion

There have been significant changes in orientation in Hong Kong's academia in the last decade, owing partly to the change of sovereignty and partly to the spread of higher education. The economic recession since 1998 has aggravated the situation, which cannot now be restored even though the economy has since improved.

Academic links between Hong Kong and China, almost non-existent prior to 1997, have flourished, especially in scientific and technological fields where ideology is not an issue. More and more of Hong Kong's incoming scholars come from the mainland, although they may be holders of doctoral degrees from prestigious universities in the West. More and more Hong Kong academicians submit their books and papers to mainland institutions for publication. Can their quality be comparable to the academic publications of the West? Is this outright discrimination or just 'politically correct' because they are published in the Chinese language? This poses a serious problem, as academic quality in the universities, and thus funding, is linked to a centralized semi-government bureau, the University Grants Committee.

The other issue is freedom of expression and speech. There are no new laws nor legal apparatus to oversee this area. However, scholars and particularly the press are much more sensitive about discussing touchy political/foreign policy (which is outside the remit of the Hong Kong SAR) issues, such as China's relations with Japan or Taiwan, or issues on Tibet. This may explain why scholars are suddenly interested in issues of local culture and society, to avoid confrontational issues, and have been extremely harsh on the SAR government, which everyone knows takes direction from China's central government in many of its political decisions. The Hong Kong SAR government has been spending huge amounts of money to fund research to boost its public and international image. The bulk is in the form of social science projects conducted under the auspices of research institutes in universities, which may have the results published as occasional papers.

There has been a great deal of pressure to publish in Hong Kong academia since 1997, with the proliferation of universities from two to eight in 15 years. Junior faculty members are now given from one to three years of contract, while universities are trying to lure retired or early-retired college professors from eminent overseas universities, as Hong Kong still pays a high salary to senior academicians. They are used as stars in a competition for enrolling quality students locally and from the mainland. Given that junior academics are driven to short-term results, self-sponsored publishing in the Chinese language has been prevalent.

Other than economic pressure, the demise of publishing in the humanities is also due to the debate over how scholarship should be measured. At this moment six out of eight university presidents (including the Hong Kong Institute of Education) have careers in the natural sciences/engineering, two in economics/business and one (at the newly founded private university) in law. In the natural science tradition, scholarship is measured through annual output of published papers; in the case of the humanities it is book manuscripts. Thus it is no wonder that many of the academic monographs published in Hong Kong are edited volumes to which every colleague in the discipline contributes an article. This may be the minimum requirement to maintain an academic license, although as a piece of published work the theme may be blurred and the contents uneven. Nonetheless, they are 'made in Hong Kong'. The university administrators tell the local press daily that they are ranked among the 50 top universities in the world, etc. This only indicates their insecurity as compared with their salaries. The question is: are these folks providing quality education to Hong Kong's next generation?

3

Scholarly communication in Japan
Hitoshi Kamada

Much like any other country, Japan has developed unique cultural aspects that have colored its scholarly communication practices. This chapter describes some of the unique aspects of scholarly communication in Japan, offering an overview of the history and current state of Japanese scholarly activities as well as other related issues such as copyright. It also discusses recent changes and future developments in Japanese scholarly communication.

Development of academic systems

History prior to 1868

Japan has a long history of scholarly pursuits dating back to ancient times, when the earliest form of Japanese civilization took shape. Initially, Chinese civilization had a significant influence on ancient Japan. Japanese envoys to China during the Tang dynasty (630–894) contributed greatly to bringing the fruits of Chinese civilization to Japan. Japanese Buddhist monks engaged in religious studies with an emphasis on Chinese forms of worship and theology, and Japanese aristocrats studied Chinese literature for their education, enlightenment and pleasure. The study of Chinese literature, religion, social systems and so forth was the major focus of Japanese scholarly activities at that time. And yet, simultaneously, Japan began to develop its own unique, distinctive culture. A uniquely Japanese literary style, new Japanese Buddhist sects and other characteristically Japanese styles within the arts and humanities began to emerge.

Additional contributors to and influences upon the development of Japanese civilization arrived in the sixteenth century, when several Western countries, notably Spain and Portugal, made contact with Japan. In particular, firearms from the West drastically changed the shape and outcomes of Japanese medieval wars. After the country's unification under a Tokugawa lord, Japan closed its shores and forswore all contact with other countries, except for limited interactions with China, Korea and the Netherlands. This closed state during the Edo period (1603–1867) remained in effect for more than 200 years.

During the Edo period, under the Tokugawa family's feudal regime, scholarly activities flourished in various disciplines, such as history, medicine and mathematics. Scholarly activities were initially monopolized by the warrior classes. They developed a system of ethics unique to their place in Japanese society that justified and legitimized their control of the government and culture, and they passed their beliefs and ethics on to their children. The ruling Tokugawa regime established a school, called *Shōheikō*, for the ruling clans. The school's mission was to foster top-class bureaucrats who would govern the country to the benefit of the regime. At the same time, local lords who came under the control of the Tokugawa family started their own schools for the warrior class, especially after the middle of the Edo period. These schools taught primarily ethics for warriors, but some taught more practical subjects like medicine and sciences. Additionally, some schools began to offer classes on new medical techniques and technologies imported from the West and made available to the Japanese through limited contact with traders from the Netherlands.

In tandem with the schools for the ruling and warrior classes, many private schools came into being. These schools emerged first in large cities like Osaka, which at the time was an important center of economic activity, and soon spread across the country. They attracted students not only from the privileged ruling and warrior clans, but also from other classes, including mercantile families. Eager-to-learn students sought to study under prominent masters in their chosen disciplines; and the good reputation of these schools spread and attracted more students. These private schools were more focused on pure scholarly pursuits than the schools for the warrior classes that produced bureaucrats. By the end of the Edo period, Japanese medical schools specializing in European medical techniques had produced many doctors with Western medical skills. A more scientific approach to scholarship with a new basis in the review of written materials took off.

The result of the creation and success of various schools was a country that could boast one of the world's highest literacy rates among its population at that time. A strong appetite for reading among the literate public supported the proliferation of publishing houses and the spread of literature. Book printing became widespread, and many people enjoyed access to printed materials like popular novels. During this period of civil tranquility, cities like Edo (which was later to become Tokyo) became major cosmopolitan centers, and commercial activity increased dramatically. Consequently, the mercantile classes prospered. Children from non-warrior or noble families attended school to study reading, writing and calculus – the necessary skills for success in commerce.

The new technologies, disciplines and knowledge, coupled with increased critical thinking among students, led some to question the existing social structure. A growing interest in the study of European civilization fed a popular movement calling for the end of the government's long-term policy of a closed Japan. Many students who enrolled in private schools and subsequently developed keen critical faculties were later instrumental in the toppling of the Tokugawa regime.

Birth of universities

A transitional period, commonly known as the Meiji Restoration, followed the fall of the Tokugawa regime in 1867, with popular pressure to open Japan to the rest of the world acting as one of the major forces that toppled the regime. It was during the Meiji Restoration that the country opened itself to Western civilization and began its rapid transition from feudal regime to modern, industrialized nation. A strong interest in and appreciation of aspects of Western civilization emerged; and as a result the newly reformed Japanese government created and implemented a system of modern higher education based on the Western college-centered model, and characterized by government-run imperial universities. The high education level and literacy rate already existing in Japan prior to the establishment of the university system made possible a relatively quick transition to the new model of higher education.

The University of Tokyo was the first modern-era university to be established. It was founded in 1877 and grew from the union of an academy of the previous Edo regime founded in 1856 and a medical school established in Tokyo in 1858. In 1886 this school became the Imperial University. In subsequent years additional imperial universities came into being; an example is the Kyoto Imperial University. The organizational structure of the imperial universities, which were based on the structure of the Tokyo Imperial University, became the foundation of the modern higher education system.

While strong government initiatives created a base for the development of the higher education system during the Meiji period, the imperial universities were not the sole option for collegiate study. Several prominent individuals (like Yukichi Fukuzawa, an educator and enlightenment thinker) founded private schools offering a modern, Western-style education. These schools eventually became prominent private universities, including Waseda University and Keio University in Tokyo. At the same time, a number of vocational schools for the training of legal professionals emerged. In 1918, by a law establishing a formalized university system in Japan, the private schools and some of the vocational schools became recognized as private universities and an integral part of the national higher education system. The same law also called for the creation of new public universities to supplement the imperial universities. By 1940 the total number of universities had reached 47, with a total enrollment of over 80,000 students.

From the beginning, it was common practice to invite scholars, doctors, engineers and so forth from the West. These people brought with them the skills and knowledge that Japan needed to modernize rapidly. Even prior to the Meiji Restoration, Western foreigners traveled to Japan, bringing with them and transferring to the Japanese their expertise. Notable among them were Erwin von Bälz of Germany, who taught medicine, and Edward Sylvester Morse of the USA, who contributed to the development of the study of archaeology and anthropology in Japan. Initially, the foreign scholars were instrumental in the growth of scholarly disciplines in Japan. However, as the nation advanced technologically and the rate of social change stabilized, Japanese scholarship matured and began to produce remarkable results relatively independent of Western guidance. This vigorous new academic environment also began to foster a more liberal, critical way of thinking, which enjoyed its zenith in a democratic movement during the Taishō period (1912–1926). For example, one prominent constitutional scholar produced works that challenged the sovereignty of the emperor within the Japanese constitutional framework. However, as Japanese governmental systems and structures gradually morphed into imperialism, this nascent movement toward a more populist form of governance was stifled.

The contemporary higher education system

After the Second World War universities were reorganized and subsumed into a new national system of higher education. The former imperial universities became national universities, in the same classification as other national universities that were not a part of the imperial group. The private universities that existed before the war continued to operate, and former private vocational schools expanded to became true universities. Nevertheless, despite the post-Second World War restructuring, the former imperial universities remain pre-eminent within the national university system, and it is generally believed that the former imperial universities, along with certain select public universities, are more prestigious than most private universities. They attract the highest quality of applicants, and their academic output and presence are deemed to be more significant than those of other universities. They boast far more graduates in high positions in politics, government, the legal profession, medicine, business and other disciplines and specialties. The years subsequent to the Second World War saw the proliferation of new universities and colleges, buoyed by the growing demand for mass higher education as Japan recovered from the ruin of the war and emerged as an international economic powerhouse. Today, there are over 700 universities in Japan.

In recent years the country has begun to experience the more immediate effects of a declining number of young adults among its population. This has forced universities to compete to attract the best candidates from among an increasingly smaller pool of students. Some universities, particularly the newer, less prestigious private universities, are having trouble attracting the minimum number of students required to operate effectively. At the same time, public universities have had to deal with tighter government funding. The collapse of the overheated economy of the late 1980s rendered the Japanese economy sluggish during the entire decade of the 1990s. Stagnant and inflexible economic and governmental systems were blamed, among other factors, for the slow recovery. Faced with massive debts and deficits, the Japanese government restructured various systems in an effort to curtail spending and improve efficiency. Under this restructuring, higher education funding was carefully scrutinized. As private universities rely heavily on government support, the lower funding levels, when coupled with reduced revenue due to low student enrollment, could take a severe toll on private universities.

Under the restructuring, national universities became government agencies. Reorganized as independent administrative agencies, they now have more independence from the national government, but fewer guaranteed funding commitments. The combination of reduced government funding and increased administrative independence has forced the former national universities to run their institutions more effectively and efficiently. As a result, both public and private universities have initiated reforms in areas like admission, curriculum, organizational structure, student services and so forth. In an effort to adapt to broad societal changes, more universities are offering new interdisciplinary programs like information science, cultural studies, international studies, public policy and management. These programs are offered partly in response to increased popular demand for practical higher education that helps students find employment in a competitive job market within an increasingly global economy, but are also the result of a new maturity in scholarly research in Japan. Increasingly, scholars are reaching beyond the traditional boundaries of their research areas toward interdisciplinary studies.

Along with undergraduate education, graduate professional schools have flourished in recent years. In the past, students entering graduate schools (with some exceptions, like medical schools) almost always intended to pursue academic careers. This custom was encouraged by companies' common practice of lifetime employment, under which employers hire graduating undergraduates and train them with company resources in their particular corporate culture, which makes an extensive and potentially expensive sojourn in graduate school impractical for most undergraduates. Additionally, many companies set age limits for prospective employees, which make any postponement of entry to the workforce unwise. In recent years, however, the employment process has become more forgiving and more fluid. While the lifetime employment custom is still practiced, more people now move from one workplace to another, either voluntarily (seeking better employment) or mandatorily (as a result of layoffs). More people seek temporary jobs, and remain temporarily employed for longer periods. Faced with intense competition, and under pressure to streamline their workforce, corporations are increasingly willing to hire skilled workers trained elsewhere for immediate deployment of their talents. The result of all of these changes has been to make professional graduate school a more attractive option for graduating college students. Many university graduates now enroll in graduate school after several years of employment. Newly created graduate schools of business administration have been one response to this new demand for graduate education. In addition, changes in the legal system have resulted in the creation of graduate law schools (a graduate legal degree was not previously required for entrance to the legal profession, as the system was based solely on entry examinations). As the demand for higher education increases and becomes more diverse, requiring new areas of specialization, scholarly communication will further evolve.

Development of academic professions and culture

The historical development of the academic professions has resulted in some unique practices and customs in Japanese academia, and has strongly influenced the manner in which scholars communicate today. Prior to the Second World War, imperial universities employed an organizational structure based on clusters called *kōza* to organize faculty, with *kōza* assigned to individual major disciplines. A full professor headed each *kōza*, and associate and assistant professors belonged to *kōza* as the *kōza* head's subordinates. The *kōza* served as the basic unit through which research was pursued and education was delivered in each disciplinary area.

The *kōza* system encouraged the development of a seniority-based hierarchy among the faculty of universities. The legacy of this system remained prevalent in the former imperial universities after the Second World War, and similar organizational dynamics have become common in other universities and colleges that adopted the *kōza* structure. Unfortunately, the *kōza* system encouraged the growth of a rigid, hierarchical and ultimately stagnant culture at universities. Additionally, the more practical problem of aligning research specialties with teaching areas by *kōza* surfaced. In response to these issues, a new organizational structure assigning faculty members to major educational areas without any hierarchical structure or designation came into being after the war.

Whether or not the *kōza* system exists within an institution, graduate students traditionally have something similar to a mentor-apprentice relationship with their professors. This is reminiscent of the old tradition of learning wherein students enroll in a school and become apprentices of the teacher. Professors have tremendous influence over student admissions to graduate programs in their disciplines, and play a continuous role as mentors over the course of students' graduate careers. Graduate students will often choose to apply to a particular school with the intention of pursuing graduate study under a preferred professor. Subsequently, the professor will advise his or her students not only on how to proceed with research but where to publish. Traditionally, this same professor will help his or her students find jobs, either through the professor's influence within his or her own institution or through personal connections in other institutions.

The close relationship between professor and graduate student, with the prospect of employment gained through the influence of the senior professor's personal network, dominates much of a graduate student's academic career. This sort of relationship remains customary in more traditional academic departments such as literature and history. They tend to be departments within which only a small number of graduate students per faculty are admitted and class size remains small. However, the newer graduate schools teaching interdisciplinary subjects and offering professional training are quite different. In these schools the ratio of graduate students to teaching faculty is much larger, and the traditional mentor-apprentice relationship is far weaker.

The government-led systematization of the universities after the Meiji Restoration preceded the development of independent academic societies, and the dearth of forums within which to share knowledge and research made universities the primary locus for academic communication and knowledge exchange. A further consequence was that universities came to publish their own journals and create academic societies based within institutions. The result was to engender a greater loyalty among professors to the institutions to which they belong, rather than to the disciplines in which they specialize.

While the practice of lifetime employment has declined within some corporations in recent years, universities have more or less retained this tradition. The practice further reinforces professorial loyalty to institutions before disciplines. Many universities hire faculty from their pool of graduate students; these students-cum-professors subsequently remain employed by those same institutions for the duration of their entire careers. In recent years the mobility of professors between institutions has increased. More universities advertise faculty positions openly to the public and hire scholars with degrees from institutions other than their own. Nevertheless, employment referrals through the teacher-student relationship, or via personal connection created by institutional ties, still influence faculty hiring and employment practices.

While many professors in the sciences, technology and medicine (STM) possess doctoral degrees, it is rare that institutions grant doctorates in the humanities and social sciences. Doctoral degrees in these disciplines are usually granted to experienced professors with significant achievements. Doctoral students in the humanities and social sciences generally find employment after completing all course requirements without the granting of a degree, or even while they are still enrolled in a doctoral program. In recent years, however, the granting of doctoral degrees to graduate students in these disciplines has been encouraged by the government.

The appointment of college and university professors generally begins at the *kōshi* (lecturer) or *joshu* (assistant) level. After several years' experience, *kōshi* and/or *joshu* are promoted to *jokyōju*. Literally, *jokyōju* means assistant professor, but this rank is generally considered to be the equivalent of an associate professorship in the USA. *Kyōju*, the next step up, denotes the rank of full professor. In 2007 the government implemented a number of changes in the faculty ranking system, including the creation of the rank of *junkyōju* (associate professor), which replaces the rank of *jokyōju*.

While universities follow the practice of lifetime employment, they do not have a true tenure system. Once a professor is hired at the entry level, he or she may remain in the same institution for the rest of his or her career. Unlike universities in the USA, there is no mandatory tenure review after several years of employment. Still, an evaluation prior to promotion to associate or full professor is required. While exact criteria for promotion vary by institutions, the number of publications plays an important part. Notwithstanding the guarantee of lifetime employment, however, most universities do have a mandatory retirement policy. Public universities set a mandatory retirement age earlier than private universities, with 60 as the usual retirement age. Often prominent scholars retired from public universities find employment at private universities and colleges.

Scholarly publishing formats

The publication of original research is an integral part of academic activities and is an important means of communication for the advancement of scholarship. While online publications are emerging, print remains the primary medium for scholarly publications. Academic publishing also entails the publication of primary resources for research, especially in art, literature and history. Japan's long and rich history is marked by the writing of numerous significant documents; the packaging and publishing of these sources for a scholarly and popular readership are active.

Monographs

The state of scholarly monograph publishing

The exact number of scholarly books published is unknown, primarily because there is no exact definition of what constitutes a scholarly book. Scholarly books may be defined as monographs published for the purpose of disseminating scholarly information (including new knowledge within a specific theme or for the integration of previous research within a wider theme), for the presentation and explanation of basic knowledge within a particular field to new students or researchers, or for entirely different reasons. Any monograph intended for scholars, students and specialists in a specific discipline may be considered to be a scholarly book. One may consider any book published by a scholarly publisher like a university press to be a scholarly book. Books that are considered by some to be scholarly may not have a bibliography or reference list, a primary criterion for scholarly publications. With these caveats in mind, research published in 1987 estimated the number of scholarly monographs published in Japan at that time to be between 5,900 and 8,300 per year (Mushakoji, 1987). This was about 9–13 per cent of the total published monographs per year.

University presses, commercial publishers and academic societies all publish scholarly monographs. Governmental agencies and private research institutes also publish a certain number of scholarly monographs every year. In addition, some scholarly books are self-published. Universities that do not have their own university press nevertheless may also publish monographs occasionally. Scholarly monographs are more common in the humanities and social sciences, while journals are the preferred format for publishing research in the sciences, technology and medicine, as rapid dissemination of new research results is crucial in those fields. Most scholarly monographs are published in initial runs of several hundred copies.

Commercial publishing

The publishing industry has experienced a recent downturn. While publishing houses are putting out a growing number of titles, their sales are stagnant. A unique Japanese practice, called *saihan-seido*, allows retail booksellers to return unsold books to publishers, which creates a large back catalog and cuts into publisher profits. Under this system, books are sold at the same price everywhere. This controversial practice is now being re-examined in an effort to facilitate and increase competition within the publishing industry. A more detailed discussion of the publishing and retail bookselling industries is beyond the scope of this chapter.

The combination of the resale system and resale price maintenance system may have been beneficial to the distribution and sale of scholarly books, which are generally not as profitable as publications for the popular market, to general bookstores. Academic libraries are major buyers of scholarly books, and their purchases augment the sales of such books to individuals at retail bookstores, increasing overall profitability. The publication of academic books is also subsidized by the sale of textbooks, by government and institutional grants, and even by purchase of extra volumes by the author, who then resells the books on an individual basis.

University press publications

Twenty-seven university presses currently belong to the Association of Japanese University Presses. Other university presses exist that are not members of this association. Only a very few universities operate presses. However, the number of university presses has increased a little in recent years; in turn, the number of university press publications is also increasing. Some university presses are particularly active. One of the largest, the University of Tokyo Press, prominently advertises its new publications in national newspapers. All the same, most university presses remain small in size and publish only a few titles each year. Consequently, the total output of university presses does not constitute the majority of scholarly monograph publishing.

The high quality of publications from university presses is generally assumed from the good reputation of the university with which the press is associated. The respect and pre-eminence accorded to a university are in turn accorded to the publications of its press. The quality of university publications is also presumed from the low number of titles published every year by university presses, as it is generally believed that this low number stems from an attention to detail in each publication made possible by the limited quantity of titles. However, if the numbers of university presses and their publications increase, independent verification of the high quality of each title may become necessary.

Scholarly books for the general audience

In addition to pure scholarly monographs, numerous titles are published each year aimed at the general public and intended for the non-specialist, non-expert reader. Shortly after the creation of the company in 1913, Iwanami Shoten, now one of the most prestigious publishers in Japan, grew as a major scholarly publishing house. In 1927 it began to publish a series of general education books in paperback format. This series, called Iwanami Bunko, was the first instance of a now vastly popular Japanese paperback genre called *bunko*. In subsequent years Iwanami Bunko titles have included republications of influential scholarly works, classical texts and masterpieces by prominent historical figures. The Iwanami Bunko series has since its inception grown into an extensive catalog of works from around the world, including Greek philosophy, Chinese poetry, etc. Other publishers have since followed suit in publishing their own *bunko* series of general education paperbacks, and these are now available in bookstores across the nation at reasonable prices that many people can afford. The success of the *bunko* genre proves the existence of a large readership for general education materials.

It is common for university professors in Japan to write books on their areas of expertise for a general, non-specialist readership in addition to publishing scholarly works. These generalist works are published by mainstream publishers for non-academic readers and written in an easy-to-read style, usually with minimal references. Some of these books take the form of a conversation with one or more scholars on a scholarly subject, as the narrative text of these conversations is easy for non-specialists to follow. As these books are published by large general publishers, they are distributed more widely than typical scholarly books, and some make the national bestsellers lists. For example, a renowned scholar of Japanese language, Susumu Ōno, published a book titled *Nihongo Renshū-chō* (*The Japanese Workbook*). It became the second-highest bestselling book in Japan for 1999. These appealing mixtures of the scholarly and popular are prominently displayed in retail bookstores. Published in hardback as well as soft-cover format, the better-selling hardback titles are often republished in paperback format.

Other popular book genres in Japan include historical novels, fictionalized accounts of the lives of historical figures and novelizations of events in Japanese history. Numerous archaeological sites and new discoveries in Japan have stimulated a strong interest in archaeology among the public. This particular aspect of history is so popular among the Japanese that non-professional scholars are a common sight at lectures by historians and at newly discovered archaeological sites. Books on the Japanese language and linguistics are also extremely popular, as the Japanese are keen to learn the correct language usage required for proper social interactions and rituals. The popularity of this particular genre reflects a general concern with new words, changing grammar usage and new conversational styles that are taking over traditional forms of discourse in quotidian Japanese life.

Scholarly journals

Kiyō journals

The most notable and unique characteristic of scholarly journal publication is the prevalence of *kiyō*. *Kiyō* are journals published by universities, departments within a university or academic societies based in a particular university department (in contrast to scholarly monographs, which are generally published by university presses). *Kiyō* are particularly predominant in the humanities and social sciences; they are also published in the sciences, technology and medicine, although their role in STM scholarly communications is limited. *Kiyō* came into being in the Meiji period (1868–1912) when Japan implemented a modern university system based on the European university model. At that time, *kiyō* resembled monographic serials, as each issue featured a single work by a single author. In subsequent years *kiyō* evolved into their current incarnation as house journals published by universities and their departments. The number of *kiyō* grew larger after the Second World War, corresponding to the increase in the number of universities/colleges and their academic departments.

Customarily, universities and colleges publish *kiyō* in small print runs and trade individual issues for *kiyō* issues from other institutions. Some of these traded issues are added to university library collections. They are not available through mainstream publication distribution channels like bookstores or distributors. For some *kiyō* the publication cycle is irregular, and many *kiyō* are published only once a year or even less. For these reasons *kiyō* are considered gray literature, despite the fact that they comprise a majority of journal publishing in the humanities and social sciences.

Some *kiyō* do not cover specific disciplines exclusively, as the departments publishing them may include different disciplines. *Kiyō* published by such departments may include articles on many different subjects in a single issue. This makes their target audience diffuse and any objective evaluation of submitted articles difficult. In fact, *kiyō* generally do not have any established selection criteria or submission guidelines. *Kiyō* are often criticized and dismissed by some scholars and others due to the fact that any member of the faculty belonging to the department publishing the *kiyō* may publish whatever they want in that *kiyō* without any prior peer review. Consequently, some *kiyō* articles are of decidedly poor quality. The irregular quality of *kiyō* articles, coupled with their limited visibility, has prompted many scholars to claim that no one reads *kiyō* articles. Nevertheless, one can find high-quality articles published in obscure *kiyō*.

Some *kiyō* issues include articles called *kenkyū nōto* (research notes). These are articles on research in progress, or informal accounts of one's ongoing research. Drawing a distinction between *kenkyū nōto* and full research articles is often an arbitrary matter. Graduate students may publish their first articles in *kiyō* as *kenkyū nōto* or full-length research articles. Often, senior professors will arrange the publication of articles by graduate students in departmental *kiyō*. In this manner, *kiyō* help young scholars build up their publishing records.

Academic society journals

Academic society journals in the humanities and social sciences are quite small in number, particularly when compared to *kiyō*. The number of nationwide academic societies in the humanities and social sciences is quite small. In fact, many academic societies are based in specific institutions, and the journals published by these societies are considered to be *kiyō* and not true society journals. Not all society journals, even those published by national societies, use a peer-review process or have established selection criteria for publication. Membership fees are the primary source of funding, but inadequate revenues from membership fees have put a strain on society journal publishing. In addition to their limited number, publishing in society journals is no more advantageous than publishing in *kiyō* for purposes of faculty hiring and promotion in the humanities and social sciences. Consequently, many scholars are content with publishing their articles in *kiyō* and may forgo society journal publication altogether.

Commercial involvement in scholarly journal publishing

Commercial academic journals have little presence in Japanese academia, especially in the humanities and social sciences. The predominance and pre-eminence of *kiyō* obviate any need for commercial scholarly journals. This is in contrast with countries like the USA, where commercial publishers have largely taken over scholarly journal publication. Thanks to this, Japanese academic libraries have yet to experience the steep inflation of scholarly journal subscription prices seen in the USA. Nevertheless, Japanese academic libraries have felt the sting of rapidly inflating scholarly journal prices in the prohibitively high cost of acquiring access to journals sold overseas, like the STM journals sold by Elsevier. This state of affairs has also largely impeded a transition from traditional print publishing to the electronic publishing model, enabled rapidly elsewhere by commercial publishers. The lack of major commercial players and the existence of numerous smaller publishers involved in scholarly journal publishing seem to have slowed the advancement of electronic scholarly journal publishing.

STM journals

After the Second World War Japanese scientists assembled an impressive roster of achievements in STM, and research in these areas remains very active. Both private and public sectors have directed considerable funding to scientific research. Scholarly communications in STM are global: this enables researchers from all over the world to share research results, which in turn allows more immediate advances in scientific pursuits and practical applications universally. As a result, STM scholarly communication practices are closer to international norms than in the humanities and social sciences.

Most major Japanese STM journals are society publications. Some Japanese STM societies are big enough to sustain a large professional readership, and more STM society journals employ the peer-review/referee process than those in the humanities and social sciences. Impact factors, which look at the average number of cited journals in an article, are more widely employed by STM societies in evaluating scholarly journals. Many researchers use STM journals published overseas and submit articles written in English for publication. More Japanese STM journals are beginning to include abstracts and/or articles written in English in order to appeal to a foreign readership.

Electronic publishing

Japanese electronic publication of scholarly works is most prominent in the digitization of scholarly journals, with the electronic publication of

Japanese STM journals growing rapidly. Recently the Japan Science and Technology Agency launched a website called J-STAGE (Japan Science and Technology Information Aggregator), through which the electronic full text of articles published in Japanese STM journals is available. The National Institute of Informatics (NII), a government agency charged with facilitating access to scholarly information, has recently launched SPARC-Japan, a Japanese version of a US-originated project (Scholarly Publishing and Academic Resources Coalition). One of the primary objectives of SPARC-Japan is to help make Japanese research more accessible to a wider scholarly readership through initiatives like partnerships with publishers and offers of support for the development of electronic publications by Japanese research institutions. Over 1,000 society journals are available through the NII's electronic library, which is linked from its Scholarly and Academic Information Navigator, also called CiNii.

The digitization of journals in the humanities and social sciences is proceeding more slowly. Nevertheless, several society journals in these areas are now available electronically through CiNii, and the number is steadily growing. In addition, more universities are now digitizing their *kiyō* and making them available electronically through websites or more advanced institutional repositories. The NII has started a project in collaboration with universities across the country for the development of academic content infrastructure and institutional repositories at universities across the nation. Currently, the NII is collaborating with 40 institutional repositories.

Electronic scholarly books remain scarce, even as academic libraries provide access to electronic books published overseas through such platforms as NetLibrary. A plausible explanation for the scarcity of scholarly electronic books may be the lack of real interest in electronic books among scholars and a strong preference for continued use of the print format. Additionally, academic publishers have yet to encounter any really strong incentive to commence regular publication of electronic monographs. All the same, popular interest in print-on-demand materials is growing steadily – an interest that is more easily served through electronic publication and printing. Because print-on-demand allows publishing houses to print smaller runs, the potential exists for greater demand for the electronic publication of scholarly monographs which would otherwise not be sufficiently profitable to warrant printing the number of copies involved in a traditional print run. Once formatting standards are established and accepted, electronic publishing may well prove to be the publication model that eases the cost of publishing scholarly monographs.

Some academic publishers that previously made primary resources available to researchers and scholars through microform publication are now actively engaged in digitizing primary resources and making them available on CD-ROM or DVD. The enhanced capabilities of CD-ROMs and DVDs, such as navigation and viewing which are not available in print or microform formats, add value to these primary resource products. However, some fear that these electronic formats may be superseded, and question their continued viability and value as a primary format for long-term preservation. In any case, publishers have yet to offer many online or web-based scholarly products. Many academic publishers do not have sufficient capital to invest in starting and maintaining these products. In their place, many academic institutions and museums are digitizing their primary resources and making them available on the web. Examples include historical artworks and literary texts – the Japan Center for Asian Historical Records has generated over 12 million images of historical materials.

The dearth of web-based electronic databases available from Japanese publishers is distressing to foreign scholars, and to libraries specializing in Japanese studies and eager to include online electronic resources on Japan in their collections of electronic resources. Exacerbating the problem is the reluctance of Japanese database vendors to offer their products for sale to foreign purchasers. The database vendors have been slow to revise their licensing clauses to meet the needs of overseas users. One example that is particularly aggravating to would-be overseas purchasers is the fact that licensing agreements for Japanese databases typically include a clause stipulating that if any legal dispute involving the licensing or use of the database should arise, that dispute will be adjudicated in a Japanese court. Most overseas users cannot or will not accept such a requirement. Additionally, many Japanese database vendors do not consider the labor involved in licensing negotiation worth the bother, as the overseas markets remain small in contrast to the domestic market. Consortial purchases of electronic databases by academic libraries are not yet common practice in Japan, and Japanese database vendors hesitate to negotiate licensing agreements with library consortia overseas. Yet there is recent evidence that vendors are becoming more willing to accommodate the circumstances of overseas users.

Other aspects of scholarly communication

Copyright

Copyright is a complex subject, and any detailed discussion of it is beyond the scope of this chapter. The description here is by no means a rigorous legal discussion, and only touches on several notable points. Japan has a well-established copyright law and has attained a standard for copyright protection comparable to that of other nations through its compliance with the Berne Convention for the Protection of Literary and Artistic Works, under which copyright is automatically accorded to original works. Under this convention, any materials originating in Japan are protected in all countries that are convention signatories, under said countries' copyright law. In turn, materials created in other Berne Convention signatory countries that are subsequently used in Japan are protected under the Japanese copyright law.

In Japan, works are copyright protected for the life of the creator and 50 years after the creator's death. In contrast, copyright protection extends to 70 years after the death of the creator in the USA and many European nations. An extension of Japanese copyright protection to 70 years after the death of the creator in order to bring Japanese law in line with the international norm is currently being debated. A notable aspect of Japanese copyright law, unlike US copyright law, is its prominent stipulation of a 'moral right of the author' in Articles 18–20. For example, Article 20 states: 'The author shall have the right to preserve the integrity of his work and its title against any distortion, mutilation or other modification against his will.' These specific 'moral right' provisions have a profound effect on how illustrations, summaries and quotations from others' work are used in scholarly publications.

As in other countries, the Japanese copyright law allows exceptions for the use of copyrighted materials without the prior permission of the creator. Under US copyright law, 'fair use' allows the use of copyrighted materials 'for purposes such as criticism, comment, news reporting, teaching (including multiple copies for classroom use), scholarship, or research'. Japanese law, in contrast, does not contain a similar, general, fair-use provision. Instead, it makes provisions for specific circumstances, such as reproduction for private use, reproduction in libraries and quotations. For example, by a provision specific to reproductions of library materials, a photocopy of a library-owned book for research purposes is allowed, provided that said photocopy is of only a portion of the book. While the provision does not specify what percentage of a book constitutes a 'portion', it is customary for Japanese libraries to allow the reproduction of no more than half of a book.

Copyright is properly observed in general popular publishing and media; however, the handling of copyright can sometimes be lax in Japanese scholarly publishing. The value of scholarly publications as a conduit for the dissemination of scholarly findings appears to have overshadowed the copyright of the authors in the material they create. Scholarly publications by non-commercial publishers are particularly lax about copyright. Many scholarly journals, especially *kiyō*, do not include clear notes on who retains the copyright of articles submitted for publication, as they often lack formal submission guidelines. Moreover, many scholarly journals do not explicitly ask for a transfer of copyright from the author to the publisher. This in effect means that the author retains the copyright of his or her scholarly articles as creator of the works under Japanese copyright law. In scholarly monograph publishing, publication does not usually involve copyright transfer, and publishers merely obtain permission from authors for a one-time publication/printing. This is also true for general, non-scholarly book publication. It is common in Japan for a novel published in hardback by one publisher to be republished in paperback in a later year by a different publisher.

Making digitized journal articles available on the internet requires a separate copyright permission from copyright holders. The Japanese copyright law has specific provisions regarding the right to broadcast copyrighted materials to the public. Consequently, in order to republish scholarly articles in an electronic format while complying with the law, some journals now ask authors to sign a legal document specifically stating the author's permission for electronic republication. In addition, Japanese STM journals are beginning to ask authors explicitly for copyright transfer to publishers, in order to enable the republication of the content of their journals with greater ease. Unfortunately, current Japanese copyright law does not effectively address such new issues as the reproduction of print materials for storage in an electronic database or depository. In addition to calling for a modification to the copyright law, involved parties are now discussing how to deal with copyright issues in electronic reproduction.

Overseas scholarly communications

Historically, Japan has been eager to learn from foreign countries, like China in ancient times and Western countries in the recent past.

Especially after the Meiji Restoration, many scholars traveled to Western countries to pursue advanced studies. This tradition continues today, not only among STM scholars who need to keep abreast of new research all over the world, but also among scholars in the humanities and social sciences who are keen to learn more about the progress of research within their disciplines in foreign countries.

University professors often take sabbatical leave to spend a year or more overseas pursuing their research. In fact, quite a few professors have received advanced degrees from foreign universities. Scholars often travel overseas to attend conferences and learn about the latest research trends in their disciplines. Some Japanese universities offer residency programs to attract foreign scholars to their institutions to give seminars, lecture series and so forth. Additionally, there is great interest among undergraduate and graduate students alike in studying overseas.

Acquisition of foreign scholarly materials has been active in many disciplines. Scholarly foreign works in translation have played an important role in Japan in the dissemination of new knowledge from other countries. Translation is considered to be a notable and valuable contribution to scholarship, and many scholars translate foreign scholarly publications and primary source materials for the benefit of the Japanese academic community and the general public. Translations of important foreign works, both old and recent, are often published as monographs.

While Japan's appetite for foreign scholarly works is strong, Japanese scholars in the humanities and social sciences are yet to be as enthusiastic in the dissemination of their research overseas as in their consumption of foreign research. Language is a barrier for many. In addition, scholars in some domestic disciplines, such as Japanese history and literature, do not think much of communicating with overseas researchers. This is regrettable, as more exchanges between Japanese and foreign scholars in the humanities and social sciences would greatly stimulate scholarly communication, and the globalization of academic research is occurring across disciplines. Certainly there is growing overseas interest in Japanese studies. Advances in Japan's STM research have accelerated the international dissemination of Japanese STM publications, which in turn has prompted Japanese journals to include abstracts and the full text of articles in English, and has also spurred the growth of electronic publishing formats that enable easy overseas access.

Academic societies

Some of the early academic societies that came into being during the Meiji period include the mathematical society Tōkyō Sūgaku Kaisha and the engineering society Kōgakukai. Kōgakukai also published one of the earliest academic society journals in Japan. The number of academic societies has increased exponentially since then, and today approximately 1,700 academic societies are currently registered with the Science Council of Japan. The traditionally strong loyalty of professors to their employing institutions first and to their disciplines second seems to have slowed the growth of large-scale national academic societies. Among the humanities and social sciences, only a few are large enough to have a membership over 1,000. Many academic societies are small and tend to specialize in a particular scholarly area; others limit themselves to a narrow geographic region. Japanese STM has a greater number of national societies, and their membership is much larger.

Most academic societies in the humanities and social sciences have very small budgets, and only a few maintain a paid staff to run the society. Many also lack funds sufficient to publish society journals with wide distribution. To support societies in their publication efforts, the University of Tokyo Press established a foundation called Gakkaishi Kankō Sentō (Center for Academic Publications Japan). Societies that cannot publish journals without assistance can outsource their publishing to this foundation. In fact, many academic societies outsource administrative work like collection of membership fees, eliminating the need to maintain an in-house staff. In keeping with their small size, the conferences they hold are also quite small. This has the merit of enabling an intimate, in-depth exchange among scholars, but limits the dissemination of conference presentations to a wider audience.

As mentioned earlier, colleges and departments within academic institutions form their own academic societies and publish *kiyō* journals. Such institution-specific societies are numerous. However, how active and how effective these institution-based societies can be remains in question. It seems that some of these societies exist only to give the university or department some prestige, and are used only for publishing *kiyō*.

Government support for scholarship and scholarly communication

The government is active on several fronts in facilitating the advancement of scholarship and scholarly communication. In particular, the Japan Society for the Promotion of Science plays a pivotal role. After the recent restructuring of Japanese government organizations, the society now operates as an independent administrative agency. It has long provided grants to individual scholars. As there are only a few private foundations offering grants for research in the humanities and social sciences, government grants from the society have been an indispensable source of support for many researchers. The society also administers a new grant program for research projects by academic institutions, called the Center of Excellence (COE) Program. It provides fellowships for young scholars and offers funding to researchers for overseas travel. Moreover, it administers numerous programs that facilitate overseas scholarly exchange by hosting international seminars and inviting foreign researchers to lecture in Japan.

The Japan Foundation is another independent administrative agency whose primary objectives are to support international cultural exchange, promote Japanese culture and stimulate overseas interest in Japan. Among various cultural and educational activities, it offers research grants to overseas scholars studying about Japan and funds to overseas libraries wishing to develop their Japanese studies collections.

Roles and state of libraries and information vendors

The state of academic libraries

Under the traditional structure of academic libraries that maintained closed stacks and complex use policies, access to scholarly materials was not always convenient for library users. While more academic libraries are now organized on the open-stack model, some still maintain closed stacks partially, which makes books less accessible and lowers visibility to students. Faculty, graduate students and certain undergraduates are granted access to the closed stacks only after formally applying for access. Unlike the libraries of public or state universities in the USA, most Japanese academic libraries are open only to the affiliated faculty, staff and students of their institutions. Most academic libraries check institutional identification cards at the entrance. When a non-affiliate user wishes to visit an academic library, that user must first bring a letter of referral from another academic library or nearby public library, along with a specific list of materials she or he wishes to consult. This closed state of affairs is partly due to the Japanese universities' traditional practice of reserving library resources for the exclusive use of their institution; however, it is also born of the practical necessity to block the flocks of high school students studying for university entrance examinations and people seeking a quiet place to read and study. Japan is a small land with a large population, and quiet places for study, reading and contemplation are scarce. Study space is at a premium for high school students in particular, for whom a high grade in the university entrance examinations is critical.

Many universities maintain departmental libraries in addition to a main central library. Departmental libraries operate independently from the main library and have their own access and loan policies. Their use is reserved primarily for faculty and graduate students in their departments. Undergraduate students and students from other departments often used to need a referral from the main library to use materials held in departmental libraries. Nowadays, more departmental libraries are accessible without referrals. Theses and dissertations are often kept in these libraries, but they generally do not accept interlibrary photocopy requests for the graduate masters' theses in their collections, and people wishing to examine a particular thesis may have to arrange to visit the library in person. Doctoral dissertations are more available through interlibrary loan; however, prior permission from authors may be required in some instances.

Professors wield control over much of the materials' selection process of university libraries. At some universities librarians play a limited role in the selection and acquisition of materials, while the faculty enjoys a much stronger voice in materials' budgets and acquisitions. Some institutions give their faculty additional budgets for individual book purchases; consequently, faculty need not rely exclusively on their library for acquiring the resources needed for research.

A graduate library degree is not required as a precursor to professional librarianship. Librarian certification programs are offered in Japanese universities as a part of the undergraduate curriculum, but the certificate is required only for public library employment and not all public libraries require it. National universities hire staff specifically for librarian positions, but many private universities do not. Most private universities rotate members of the university's general staff through various units, such as accounting and departmental offices, and assign non-library specialist staff to work in libraries as part of a periodic job rotation. This has limited the ability of professional librarians to improve access to information in their libraries proactively. Moreover, in recent years some private universities have begun outsourcing library services to private companies.

While the traditional structure of academic libraries continues to operate, they are working to ensure improved access to information and offering new services. Academic libraries now provide greater access to more Japanese electronic databases for research, and are also aggressively purchasing foreign databases in an effort to meet the high demand for foreign electronic resources in STM. They are offering more library skills instruction, and redesigning physical areas in an effort to provide interactive study space for students by introducing more computer workstations and multimedia applications. Several universities have integrated library and computer-related service functions by combining their library and information systems departments, offering seamless information and technology support to users. Reflecting these changes, some universities are renaming their libraries, calling them information services centers or media centers.

Cooperative and coordinating initiatives of libraries

The National Institute of Informatics (NII), formerly NACSIS (National Center for Science Information Systems) under the Ministry of Education, is a government agency that performs original research in information science and coordinates academic information networks around Japan. It has played a central role in establishing and encouraging interlibrary cooperation among academic libraries. Since the 1980s it has served as a bibliographic utility for academic libraries. Academic libraries share cataloging records through the NII's bibliographic database and use its ILL system for their interlibrary loan services. In recent years the NII has expanded its mission to include the development of electronic libraries and academic information portals. GeNii is its scholarly and academic information portal. It encompasses databases such as CiNii (a citation database of Japanese academic journals and electronic full-text database of academic journals, mentioned earlier), a database of grant-funded research projects, a repository of discipline-specific databases and its primary bibliographic utility database, now called Webcat. The NII is working on several projects designed to improve access to the contents of academic journals through digitization and metadata creation.

Japanese academic libraries are increasingly active in communicating with overseas institutions and developing international interlibrary loan services. The Japan Association of National University Libraries

(JANUL), in conjunction with the NII, has coordinated the development of interlibrary loan service agreements with North American and Korean libraries. Not only national universities but also other public and private universities now participate in this international initiative. Currently over 100 libraries are involved in document delivery exchanges with North American libraries, primarily through electronic transfer of journal articles. Some libraries also lend books to overseas libraries, in return for access to those libraries' collections through interlibrary loan. The North American Coordinating Council on Japanese Library Resources (NCC), a cooperative entity of Japanese studies specialists and librarians, coordinates this project for North American libraries; KERIS (Korea Education and Research Information Service) represents South Korea. In addition to this new project, the NII has long enjoyed a connection through its ILL service with the British Library Document Supply Centre.

Waseda University is one of the most prestigious private universities in Japan. Its library spearheaded international library cooperation in Japan by joining the OCLC (Online Computer Library Center), a major bibliographic utility based in the USA with member libraries in many other countries. Waseda University Library loads its MARC records to OCLC servers for shared cataloging purposes, and accepts interlibrary loan requests from overseas institutions through the OCLC system. Keio University, another prestigious private university, has also joined the OCLC interlibrary loan service. These international interlibrary loan programs have greatly improved and expanded the availability of foreign information and library materials to Japanese scholars, as well as expanding access to Japanese information and library materials for overseas scholars.

The National Diet Library has played a major role in coordinating the availability of scholarly information to scholars. In addition to its role as primary legislative research support supplier for the Japanese legislature, the National Diet Library acts as a national repository of all publications in Japan. It has collected a wide rage of publications, from government documents to popular magazines published by private companies. It requires all publishers to deposit a copy of each new publication. As a result, it boasts an extensive holding of scholarly publications. Its online public catalog has been an essential tool for searching for scholarly materials. Its scholarly holdings are available in its main library in Tokyo, and in a Kansai branch in western Japan. It also accepts interlibrary loan and photocopy requests, and makes its holdings available to overseas users through its own interlibrary loan service.

Since the end of the Second World War, the National Diet Library has compiled *Zasshi Kiji Sakuin*, an index to scholarly journal articles published in Japan. Over time, its coverage has expanded to include most scholarly journals published, including *kiyō*. It has become the essential tool for finding scholarly articles in Japan. Currently, this index is available through the National Diet Library's website free of charge.

The National Diet Library is also actively engaged in digitization. It maintains an image database of its art and artifact holdings, and has developed a full-text image database of books published in the Meiji period. Another digital project it is currently undertaking is the archiving of original electronic materials like as websites and electronic journals that have no print equivalents.

In 2002 the National Diet Library opened its Kansai branch in western Japan. This new facility was created in order to acquire more storage space for the ever-growing collection, and to serve better the needs of the general public outside the Tokyo or greater Kantō area (where the main library resides). Unlike the Tokyo main library, which functions as the national repository of Japanese publications, the Kansai branch's holdings are limited to select popularly used materials. This ensures the ready availability of materials to library users on site, through photocopy delivery or via interlibrary loan services. This branch is also engaged in interlibrary cooperation initiatives and developing its digital collections.

Private special libraries

Many private special libraries are making sizeable contributions to academic research. Many local private collections preserve historical materials reflecting the rich history of Japan. Other special libraries deal with a variety of subjects and materials not confined to historical matters. The Toyō Bunko (Oriental Library), founded in 1924, is one of the most prominent special libraries in Japan. With its extensive holdings of rare materials from all over Asia, the Toyō Bunko has become one of the largest private Asian studies research institutes in the world. While the facility and library holdings are the property of this institution, the National Diet Library has managed the library section since the end of the Second World War.

The Ōya Sōichi Library is another prominent private library. It was founded in 1971, and its collection is built on a substantial number of popular magazines and other materials collected by a journalist, Sōichi Ōya.

The holdings are indexed by personal names and subjects, and the index is published as *Ōya Sōichi Bunko Zasshi Kiji Sakuin* (*Index to Journal Articles in the Ōya Sōichi Bunko*). Its in-depth indexing of popular magazine articles that are not covered by mainstream Japanese indexes of periodical articles is of inestimable value to researchers.

Booksellers and distributors for libraries

Japanese academic institutions commonly deal with several primary booksellers or distributors to obtain the bulk of their scholarly resources. Kinokuniya and Maruzen are two of the larger players in this market. Also, numerous smaller booksellers have relations with academic institutions. These smaller booksellers sell to libraries and directly to individual faculty who have been allotted book purchase budgets for personal use. TRS (Toshokan Ryūtsū Sentā) specializes in providing services to support libraries. Its primary clientele consists of public libraries, but it also deals with some academic institutions. TRS supplies not only books and other materials, but also provides MARC records and other library-related services to client libraries. The larger companies offer an array of services and products related to the management of libraries. These include library information systems with specialized modules for acquisitions and circulation, security systems, physical processing and shelving of materials, staffing for service desks and support for digitization.

Japanese book vendors not only act as distributors of electronic databases from Japan to libraries in Japan and elsewhere, but are also active in providing foreign electronic databases to Japanese academic institutions. Many popular database packages from overseas vendors are distributed in Japan through Japanese vendors, while some foreign publishers, like Elsevier, deal directly with Japanese institutions. For example, Kinokuniya Bookstores is an agent in Japan for OCLC services. Some Japanese vendors are now making their services and products available overseas. Since 1998 TRS has partnered with the Research Library Group in the USA (which is now merging with the OCLC), and uploaded its MARC records of Japanese materials to the RLG's RLIN bibliographic utility database until 2006. A recent major new development is that Kinokuniya is now partnering with the OCLC's NetLibary to make Japanese scholarly monographs available electronically.

Antiquarian booksellers

While many used bookstores deal with popular books and comics, there are a sizeable number of antiquarian booksellers dealing primarily with scholarly books. Many are independently run small businesses that specialize in specific subjects. They have been in business for a long time, and have established reputations in their specialized areas. The Jinbo-chō district in Kanda, Tokyo, is well known for its high concentration of these antiquarian booksellers among other types of bookstores. The continued existence of these antiquarian bookstores reflects a strong appetite for scholarly materials not only among professional scholars, but also among amateur scholars and the general public wishing to study particular subjects.

In the past, university professors and students frequented local antiquarian booksellers to purchase used books at a lower price and shop for rare finds. There is still some nostalgia among the older generation of scholars for this scene. However, in recent years antiquarian booksellers of scholarly books are in decline, due to the decline of reading among students and the ready availability of used books through other channels, notably online.

Summary of issues and recent changes

While it is not possible to cover all aspects of Japanese scholarly communication practices in detail, this chapter so far has described several major aspects. The historical progress of higher education and the development of academic professions have created a unique, singular culture in Japanese academia, characterized by the devotion of university faculty to institutions before disciplines, the existence of *kiyō* and the slow growth of national academic societies. The publishing culture in Japan has created a unique environment in which scholarly publishing has flourished. Academic libraries have likewise developed a unique culture, unlike that of libraries in any other country. The consumption of foreign research has made possible many contributions to Japanese scholarship and the dissemination of scholarly information. In conclusion, here is a summary of the remaining key issues in scholarly communications in Japan.

Quality control and accountability in scholarly publication

Both promises and challenges exist for the prospects of increased quality and accountability in scholarly publishing. The Japanese academic community in the humanities and social sciences has not yet fully adopted a transparent quality control process, like a blind peer-review system. Some journals claim to use peer review for selecting articles; however, the review process is not truly blind (wherein an author and reviewer do not know each other's names). Other journals, especially *kiyō*, do not have any established review system of any sort. However, as more *kiyō* are digitized and become available online, their articles' visibility will increase and the quality will be exposed to scrutiny from a wider readership.

'Grant-in-Aid for Scientific Research', called *kaken* by Japanese scholars, has been a source of major government grant funding for scholars in all disciplines. *Kaken* grants are offered in several categories, including grants for younger scholars and in support of publication of research. Many scholars rely on this grant to conduct and publish their research. *Kaken* has been criticized, because the research results of the grant-funded projects are not easily accessible and the quality of some of the research is in question. However, the NII has started to make summaries of grant-funded project proposals and their results available through its web database of 'Grant-in-Aid for Scientific Research'.

The afore-mentioned government Center of Excellence support program has encouraged competition among universities for funding. As COE allocates money to specific research projects in universities based on demonstrated merit and excellence, it has triggered universities' and scholars' effort to publish their research more actively and demonstrate their research strength. An award of COE funding and the number of successful grant proposals receiving COE funding have become criteria for first-class research universities.

There have been several attempts to rank universities based on quality and research outputs, like the number of times publications by university faculty are cited in other works. In STM, the number of publications in international journals by faculty is becoming more important to the university's reputation. In the past, universities were ranked by the difficulty of undergraduate entrance examinations and the number of graduates successfully placed in major corporations, government, law, medicine and so forth, as well as by the more ephemeral quality of perceived prestige. Increasingly, the demonstrated, quantifiable quality of research, among other factors, is viewed as a better means of measuring the academic value or quality of universities.

Increasing presence of government initiatives

One notable aspect of Japanese scholarly communication is the weaker involvement of commercial publishers in scholarly publishing – too weak for monograph publishing. There are very few commercially published scholarly journals, particularly when compared with the number of *kiyō* and society journals. As discussed earlier, this has protected Japan from the steep price increases of academic journals faced in some Western countries like the USA. Additionally, a perceived insufficiently large commercial market seems to have delayed improvements in access to scholarly information, demonstrated by the slower growth of electronic journals. While commercial publishers overseas are aggressively offering electronic products featuring full-text access to scholarly publications, digitization efforts in Japan are mostly left to the national government and individual academic institutions. Greater improvements in scholarly communication in Japan will require greater involvement of the government and coordinated efforts of academic institutions. It is encouraging that Japanese government agencies like the National Diet Library and the NII are taking the initiative in improving access to scholarly information.

Technology adaptation in scholarly communication

The publishing industry in Japan was at first slow in adapting technological advances like the internet and mobile communications to scholarly research purposes. Fortunately, it is now making up for lost time by engaging in experimentation with different publishing and distribution models. The arrival on the scene of Amazon.com, a giant internet bookseller based in the USA, has prompted an increase in Japanese booksellers offering internet shopping. Some now offer various value-added services, such as letting customers pick up their orders at nearby convenience stores, taking advantage of the increased popularity of convenience stores as a one-stop shopping spot among the Japanese. Convenience stores are becoming a major place for selling books in addition to traditional bookstores.

Large general publishers have started delivering popular novels, comics and magazines in electronic format. Cellular phones are the most popular medium for viewing electronic contents, reflecting the Japanese fondness for these phones as an all-round device for communication, transactions of many different types and entertainment. In addition to cell phones and desktop computers, Japanese companies have developed handheld electronic book readers. While this device has not yet caught on with Japanese consumers, portable electronic dictionaries are already a popular item.

Scholarly publishing in Japan has been slow to adapt to changes in technology and has consequently missed many opportunities to improve access to scholarly information. This has been in spite of several government and cooperative initiatives in digitizing and disseminating scholarly information. Consequently, there seems to be an increasing gap in availability of electronic scholarly information between Japan and other countries. While Japan lags behind, more and more scholarly information is available electronically in the USA via e-books, e-journals and digital repositories. In Asia, China is actively engaged in digitizing scholarly books. Whether this gap in access to electronic scholarly information among nations increases or decreases in the next few years remains to be seen.

4

Scholarly communication in Korea

Joy Kim and Eun-Kyung Kwon

Korea has experienced many challenges and much turmoil throughout its history – wars, poverty, dictatorship, political corruption, ideological tension and even colonization. It has few natural resources. One resource Korea does have is its people – and their resilience, intelligence and extraordinary passion for learning. Even under the direst of circumstances, the Korean people never compromised their values or lost pride in their culture. This chapter tells a unique story about their intellectual journey across millennia – what they accomplished in the past, where they are today, how they got there and what challenges lie ahead.

General background

The Korean peninsula lies between China and Japan, and shares a small portion of its north-eastern border with Russia. Slightly smaller in size than the UK, Korea was divided into two (South Korea and North Korea) at the end of the Second World War – and it remains divided to this day. The democratic South is called the Republic of Korea (ROK), and the communist North is called the Democratic People's Republic of Korea (DPRK). South Korea occupies 45 per cent of the total land, with an estimated population of almost 50 million. Since South Korea is its subject, this chapter will hereafter refer to South Korea simply as 'Korea' and South Koreans simply as 'Koreans'.

Having experienced colonization for 35 years (1910–1945) and the devastation of the Korean War for three years (1950–1953), Korea was one of the world's poorest countries in the 1960s. Over the next three decades, however, Koreans worked hard and achieved unprecedented economic prosperity. But during the 1997 financial crisis that engulfed many Asian countries, Korea was hit especially hard and was placed under the supervision of the International Monetary Fund (IMF). Within a few years, Korea regained its economic independence and confidence. In 1996 Korea joined the Organization for Economic Cooperation and Development (OECD) as its twenty-ninth member. According to the *OECD Factbook 2006*, Korea's GDP was estimated at US$1 trillion at the end of 2004, ranking ninth among OECD members (OECD, 2006). Its per capita GDP was US$20,935. Widely acknowledged as the most densely wired information technology powerhouse in the world, Korea today has the world's highest penetration of high-speed internet access to households and highest number of internet subscribers per 100 persons. It was the first country to provide high-speed internet access from every elementary, middle and high school, and enjoys a 97.9 per cent literacy rate. Contrary to prosperous South Korea, the communist North Korea is poor and little known to the world.

Intellectual heritage

While legend places the origin of Korea all the way back to 2333 BC, the earliest states with complex political structures did not appear until the first century BC. Since then, Koreans have always maintained their political independence and ethnic identity (with the exception of the years between 1910 and 1945, when Korea was under Japanese colonial rule). The fact that all Koreans share the same language and ethnic origin gives them a strong sense of national identity, which has helped them to maintain their own distinct cultural traditions for thousands of years. Until the twentieth century Koreans traditionally looked to the advanced Chinese civilization and drew a great deal from it, but in seeking solutions to the pressing problems of the day they would often turn to their own past for understanding and resolution. They would process, enhance and apply what they learned from China to make this knowledge more useful and relevant to their own way of life. In this sense, much of Korean civilization has its roots in Chinese civilization, but Korea has its own distinct characteristics.

Before industrialization in the twentieth century, Koreans had always placed the highest value on intellectual activities while disdaining commerce and manufacturing. This has resulted in a rich cultural and intellectual heritage, some of which is recognized in UNESCO's World Cultural Heritage List. Below are a few selective examples from the UNESCO list.

Koreans were the world's foremost pioneers in printing culture. To begin with, the world's oldest woodblock printing was made in Korea. During the 1966 restoration of the Sokkatap Pagoda in the compounds of the Pulguksa Temple in Kyongju (the capital of the Silla dynasty, 57 BC–935 AD), *Mugu Chonggwang Tae Darani Kyong (Pure Light Dharani Sutra)* was discovered inside the stone pagoda. Dated at around 751, it is believed to be the world's oldest existing woodblock print. The first movable metal type was also invented in Korea in 1234, preceding Gutenberg by two centuries. Historic documents state that the work *Sangjong Kogum Yemun (Prescribed Ritual Texts of the Past and Present)* was printed with cast metal type in the year 1234; unfortunately, however, the book did not survive. The earliest verified example came to light in 1972 when the French National Library's Oriental Archives (Manuscrits orientaux, Bibliotheque nationale de France) revealed the existence of volume 2 of *Chikchi Simche Yojol (Anthology of Zen Teachings by Great Buddhist Priests)* in its collection. According to the book's postscript, the two-volume anthology was printed with movable metal type at Hungdoksa Temple in Chongju, Korea, in the seventh month of 1377 during the Koryo dynasty (918–1392). Another printing treasure is the *Tripitaka Koreana*, a collection of more than 81,340 wooden printing blocks. The *Tripitaka Koreana* is the Koryo version of the Buddhist canon, and is preserved at the historic Haeinsa Temple in the south-eastern region of Korea. Completed over a 16-year period from 1236 to 1261, the more than 52 million Chinese characters, error free, not only represent the oldest and most comprehensive Buddhist canon in existence in the world today, but are also a supreme example of the high artistic calligraphy and woodwork skills of the Koryo period.

Choson Wangjo Sillok (Annals of the Choson Dynasty) is the annual record of the Choson dynasty (1392–1910), covering each king's reign from 1392 to 1863. The annals of the last two kings, Kojong (1863–1907) and Sunjong (1907–1910), are considered part of the series although they were recorded under the control of Japan. The 1,893-volume set is considered to be the record covering the longest period of a single dynasty in the world. Nobody was allowed to read the text, not even the king, and any historiographer who leaked its contents was subject to severe punishment. These strict regulations lend great credibility to these records. The first three reigns, from 1392 to 1418, were recorded in manuscripts with excellent calligraphy. Later annals were printed with movable metal and wooden type. Although four special repositories were established in different parts of the country to preserve copies of the *Annals*, three were burned down in the Imjin Waeran (Japanese invasions) of 1592–1598. The *Annals*, originally written in classical Chinese, were translated into modern Korean in both North and South Korea. The two translations cater to different purposes and audiences, and complement each other. All of the *Annals* have been digitized and are available freely online (www.sillok.history.go.kr).

King Sejong the Great (1418–1450) of the Choson dynasty, the most revered and beloved king in Korea's history, was a patron of the arts and sciences and accomplished much during his tenure as king. He established an academic research institute called Chiphyonjon early in his reign, where the best scholars in the land from all academic disciplines gathered to pursue their research and studies. Many of the notable accomplishments during Sejong's reign are attributed to the close collaboration between the Chiphyonjon scholars and the king. Their greatest accomplishment of all was the invention of Hangul, the Korean alphabet. Until then, Koreans did not have their own writing system and relied on Chinese for their written language. Since Chinese characters could only inadequately express meanings in the Korean language and took years to master, the king and his Chiphyonjon scholars, sympathetic to the general public's desire for an easier writing system, devised a simple alphabet called Hunmin Chongum ('correct sounds for the instruction of the people') and officially promulgated it in 1446. Predominantly based upon their phonological studies, the Chiphyonjon scholars developed a theory in which the syllable is divided into initial, medial and final sounds (as opposed to the syllabic bipartite division present in traditional Chinese phonology). Hangul, as it is called now, consists of ten vowels and 14 consonants which can be combined to express almost any sound. Since Hangul can be learned in a matter of hours, it has contributed to Korea's high literacy rate and the advanced printing industry. Widely praised as one of the most scientific alphabets in the world, Hangul has been the source of great cultural pride for Koreans.

Education

Koreans are known for their extraordinary passion for education. They believe that education not only builds one's knowledge and character, but is also a short-cut to economic success. Most Koreans would not hesitate to sacrifice a great portion of their time and finances for the sake of a good education. Individual families shoulder a big share of educational expenses. Throughout high school, more than 75 per cent of education expenses are financed privately, mostly by individual families. In higher education, more than 80 per cent of expenses are funded privately. Even though the level of financial burden on Korean families is the highest among OECD countries, Korea has one of the highest rates of school enrollment.

The first higher educational institution was Kukchagam, the National University, established in 992 under King Songjong during the Koryo period (918–1392). Kukchagam was in many respects like a modern university with a number of colleges, each designed to educate children from different ranks of the aristocratic society. During the Choson dynasty Kukchagam was renamed Songgyungwan, and still exists today as Songgyungwan University. The government also established smaller educational institutions called *hyanggyo* to educate the local gentry for the civil exams that qualified them for employment in the central bureaucracy. In addition, there were private institutions called *sowon*, which were founded and supported by local scholars.

Modern schools appeared in the late nineteenth century with the influx of Western culture. Korea had been isolated from the rest of the world until 1876, when Japan forced open its ports to foreign traders. The enlightened Korean intellectuals of the time saw the urgent need to modernize and educate the people to fend off Japan's imperialistic aggression, and committed themselves to educational endeavors. At the same time, Western missionaries began establishing modern schools as part of their mission programs. Korea's very first modern school, the Wonsan Academy, was established in 1883 entirely by Koreans. By 1909 there were approximately 2,400 schools, from the elementary to the college level. Approximately one-third of them were established and run by missionaries. Two of the best private universities today, Ewha Women's University and Yonsei University, trace their origins to the early schools established by American Methodist and Presbyterian missionaries, respectively.

After the formal annexation of Korea in 1910, Japan closed many schools for fear that well-educated Koreans would be critical of the colonial government and become leaders for Korean independence. Instead, Koreans received vocational training in simple manual skills at elementary or technical schools. Middle schools were renamed high schools, implying that this was the highest available level of education for Koreans. Very few Koreans were afforded the opportunity for higher education. Koreans in higher education institutions were far outnumbered by the Japanese, whose population in Korea comprised only a fraction of the populace. In August 1945, when Korea regained its independence after Japan's surrender to the Allies, there were only 19 universities in Korea – including the Kyongsong Cheguk Taehak (established as Keijo Imperial University in 1924 by the Japanese), which later became Korea's top educational institution, Seoul National University. The Korean War (1950–1953) further devastated the land and destroyed many schools and other cultural assets. Despite all these difficulties, by 1965 the number of universities had reached 162, a 750 per cent increase in just two decades. By then, higher education was no longer limited to the élite but was also available to the general public.

Today's educational system in South Korea consists of six-year elementary schools, three-year middle schools, three-year high schools and four-year colleges and universities, which include graduate programs leading to masters' and PhD degrees. There are also two- to three-year junior colleges and vocational colleges. According to *Libraries in Korea*, published by the 2006 Seoul World Library and Information Congress National Organizing Committee, as of 2005 school attendance stood at 100 per cent at the elementary school level, 97.4 per cent at middle school level, 95.8 per cent at high school level and 71.1 per cent at college level. All elementary school graduates advance to middle school, 99.7 per cent of middle school graduates advance to high school and 82.1 per cent of high school graduates advance to college or university level (Kim, 2006). These figures place Korea among the most educated countries in the world. In 2005 Deutsche Bank Research, one of the world's leading think-tanks for trends in business, society and financial markets, placed Korea among the top six nations in terms of educational level of all adults aged 25–64 – following Germany, Canada, Switzerland, the USA and Japan (Deutsche Bank Research, 2005a, 2005b). Korea was projected to be third in the same report by 2020. According to the *OECD Programme for International Student Assessment*, a three-yearly survey of the knowledge and skills of 15-year-olds in the principal industrialized countries, Korea ranked third in math, behind Hong Kong and Finland; second in reading literacy, behind Finland; fourth in science, behind Finland, Japan and Hong Kong; and first in problem-solving (OECD, 2003a).

Universities

There are different types of institutions of higher learning: colleges and universities with four-year undergraduate programs (six years for medical and dental colleges); four-year teachers' universities; two-year junior vocational colleges; a national open university called Pangsong Tongsin Taehak (Korea National Open University); and professional schools of collegiate status, such as nursing schools and theological seminaries, with two- or four-year programs. In 2005 there were more than 400 higher educational institutions, including 175 four-year universities. These institutions enrolled 3,545,774 students; and graduate enrollment stood at 290,029, with 243,833 at the masters and 46,196 at the doctoral level. In addition, the number of professors and researchers employed by higher educational institutions was 69,201. Including graduate students, as many as 360,000 people in higher education produce most of Korea's intellectual output in the form of dissertations, articles and books. Over the past 11 years universities have been the main source of new knowledge, providing 76.47 per cent of the total scholarly output of Korea, followed by government-sponsored research centers (14.12 per cent) and businesses (8.26 per cent). Universities also provided 74.45 per cent of all primary authors, and their publications were cited most often (4.21 citations per publication). Universities employ 71.3 per cent of all PhD holders (government-sponsored research centers employ 13.7 per cent and industry employs 15.1 per cent) (Korean Educational Development Institute, 2006; Hong, 2006: 52).

In 2005 79.2 per cent of professors teaching in all higher educational institutions were holders of doctoral degrees, 33.6 per cent of whom obtained their degrees from foreign universities. The same institutions also employed 2,540 foreigners in 2005, which represented 3.7 per cent of all professors and researchers.

Scholarly associations

Along with universities, academic/scholarly associations play an important role in all stages of scholarly communication. They create, consume, publish and disseminate knowledge. By far the most common form of academic society publication is journals, although occasionally they publish books as well. Scholarly associations also hold conferences that provide venues for semi-formal or informal scholarly communication among domestic and international scholars.

According to the Korea Research Foundation's website (www.krf. or.kr), as of May 2007 there are 2,411 scholarly associations with a combined membership of over 1.11 million. In terms of disciplines,

798 associations are in the social sciences, 625 in the humanities, 276 in the medical sciences, 227 in engineering, 177 in the arts and physical education, 129 in the natural sciences and 97 are multidisciplinary. The social sciences have the largest membership with more than 320,000 members, followed by engineering with 294,704 members, the humanities with 142,311 members and the medical sciences with 140,866 members. In terms of average membership per association, engineering tops the list with 1,300 members per group. Some 61 per cent of these associations publish journals, 89 per cent of which are published five or more times a year. Eighty per cent of the associations hold conferences four or more times a year. About half of the associations present 100 or more papers a year at these conferences. Social sciences associations hold conferences most frequently, followed by the humanities. Of the associations that hold international conferences, 48 per cent do so four or more times a year and about 37 per cent of associations presented 100 or more papers at international conferences.

The Korea Association of Academic Societies (KAOAS) was established in 1997 to promote communication among its 570 members, interdisciplinary cooperation and information sharing. Since 2003 the KAOAS has been publishing a series called Hanguk Haksul Yongu ui Tonghyang kwa Chonmang (Trends and Perspectives of Academic Studies in Korea). Each volume in the series highlights three associations, providing an overview of the history of the field, research trends and future projections. Another major KAOAS project is the standardization and compilation of scholarly terms, which is crucial for interdisciplinary cooperation.

Korean studies

After national liberation in 1945, the academic community began its efforts to enhance research on Korea, looking at its history, culture and society from a fresh perspective and reflecting upon and re-evaluating past scholarship from a new nationalistic point of view. Having been freed from the domination and suppression experienced under Japan's 35-year colonization, the country increased its number of Korean studies scholars. At the same time, with the rapid proliferation of Western-trained professors in the universities, Western influences began to dominate the Korean scholarly community, raising concerns among some scholars with nationalistic views.

It was in this context that the Korean government established the Academy of Korean Studies in 1978. The aim was to pursue in-depth research on the essence of Korea's intellectual heritage by identifying and interpreting traditional Korean culture, defining the academic identity of Korean studies and cultivating able scholars with global perspectives and values. These areas had been neglected, partly as a result of Korea's rapid industrialization. The academy has endeavored to establish the true identity of Korean studies, educate specialists, build information networks devoted to Korean studies, preserve written records of Korean culture, integrate and disseminate Korean studies resources and promote ongoing research in Korean studies programs overseas. In 1980 the academy launched its Graduate School of Korean Studies to provide in-depth research and education on Korea and develop original and universal theories applicable to the world. To date the school has produced some 400 masters' and 140 doctoral degree holders in history, philosophy, language and literature, music, art history, culture, religion, political science, economics, sociology and education. These include many foreign nationals who returned to their home countries, where they hold teaching or research positions. As Korea has become a major economic player in the world, many overseas universities have become increasingly interested in offering Korean studies programs. As of May 2007, the online 'Koreanists' directory of the Korea Foundation (www.kf.or.kr) lists 3,104 Korean studies experts in 86 countries. The highest concentrations may be found in China (870 Koreanists), followed by the USA (492), the Russian Federation (253) and Japan (198).

Support for research and development

In Korea the terms 'R&D', 'scholarly information' and 'research output' usually apply to sciences, technology and medicine. This is because the country as a whole is preoccupied by its progress in these fields. Policymakers believe that these areas are the driving force in today's knowledge-based society. If Korea was a late developer in the industrial age, its ambition now is to become a leader in the twenty-first century. Surprisingly, private corporations, rather than the government, are behind most of Korea's R&D programs. In 2005 the government financed 23 per cent of all R&D expenditure (excluding humanities and social sciences), while 75 per cent came from the private sector and 2 per cent from other sources, including foreign sources. This rate of public funding is lower than that of many developed countries: China 26.3 per cent, Germany 31.14 per cent and France 37.6 per cent in 2004; the UK 32.8 per cent, Canada 33.7 per cent and the USA 29.3 per cent in 2006. The OECD average was 29.3 per cent (OECD, 2007a).

Initially, the national science and technology policies focused on the introduction, absorption and application of foreign technologies. In the 1980s, however, the emphasis shifted to national R&D projects to raise the national skill level. This led to increased public and private sector R&D investment and programs to cultivate a highly skilled workforce. Government support has focused on three areas: research in the basic sciences, efficient distribution and use of R&D resources and expanding international cooperation. In the belief that this century's knowledge-based economy is fueled by science and technology, the country has been pursuing technological independence in the key areas of telecommunications, biotechnology and new materials, while at the same time advancing research in the basic sciences.

The Korea Science and Engineering Foundation (KOSEF) was established in 1977 to promote basic science and technology in pursuit of making Korea an advanced country, with a vision of becoming 'one of the top three research support institutes in the world' to lead the development of science and technology. Its activities have been expanded to support not only basic science research but also large-scale and fundamental R&D programs. In 2006 KOSEF's budget exceeded US$1.4 billion (KOSEF, 2006).

One common index to measure Korea's investment in science and technology is the ratio between gross expenditure on R&D (GERD) and gross domestic product (GDP). In 2005 Korea ranked fourth with a ratio of 2.98 per cent. The average for all OECD countries was 2.26 per cent (OECD, 2007b). Another statistic provided by the Ministry of Science and Technology (www.most.go.kr) shows that Korea spent approximately US$27 billion (or 3.23 per cent of GDP) on R&D programs in 2006 (Hanguk Kwahak Kisul Kihoek Pyongkawon, 2007).

Another index measures the number of researchers per 1,000 working adults. Korea ranked 13 with 6.8 researchers per 1,000 at the end of 2003, ahead of the OECD average of 6.51. In terms of the number of publications, in 2003 Korea ranked 11 with 2.07 per cent of Thomson Scientific publications (Science Citation Index Expanded, Social Science Citation Index and Arts and Humanities Citation Index). American researchers ranked first, with 32.17 per cent of publications, followed by Japan (9.14 per cent), the UK (8.79 per cent), Germany (7.77 per cent) and France (5.54 per cent) (OECD, 2003b: 7–8; Yun, 2007: 111). The number of science and technology publications per million people measures the potential to create new knowledge and innovative products and technology. From 1999 to 2003 Korea ranked 26 with 301 research publications; Switzerland ranked first with 1,924 research publications. The OECD's average was 681 publications per country (Thomson Scientific, 2004, 2005). In the 2005 edition of the SCI, Korea ranked 12 with 23,515 publications (Science Citation Index, 2005). In National Science Indicators, Korea ranked 14, the same as the previous year (National Science Indicators, 2005). Over the past 11 years, 14.03 per cent of research papers by Korean scientists were published in 45 domestic journals; the remainder were published in 5,869 overseas journals (Yun, 2005).

While the humanities and social sciences draw less attention than sciences, technology and medicine, there are foundations that are devoted to supporting these fields. A few of the best known are discussed below.

Public foundations

The Korea Research Foundation (KRF) (www.krf.or.kr) is the largest and most influential organization of its kind. Established in 1981, its goal is to promote, support and enhance academic activities and elevate the level of scholarship quality in the humanities, social sciences and basic sciences. Its programs include grants and scholarships, translations, cultivation of new breeds of researchers, support of universities and scholarly associations, research evaluation, database development, international cooperation, etc. Its 2007 budget was over US$1 billion.

The Korea Foundation (www.kf.or.kr) was established in 1991 to promote a better understanding of Korea in the international community and foster global friendship. Its work includes support for Korean studies programs at overseas universities and international conferences on Korea. The Korea Foundation has helped create 77 professorial positions at 53 universities in 13 countries. In 2006 the foundation supplied 19,407 volumes of library materials to 329 institutions. It also sponsors the Korean Collections Consortium of North America, a cooperative collection development and resource-sharing library program, which will be discussed later in another context.

Private foundations

Private foundations were created with the financial backing of large conglomerate corporations to nurture smaller, often neglected associations in the social sciences and humanities fields.

The Korea Academic Research Council (formerly the Daewoo Research Foundation) has supported basic research and translations in the humanities and social and physical sciences since 1980. The research results were published as more than 600 books in the Taeu Haksul Chongso (Daewoo Scholarly Series) and distributed freely to libraries.

The Songgok Foundation (Songgok Haksul Munhwa Chaedan) was founded in 1969 to support research in the humanities and social sciences. The results are published in the annual *Songgok Nonchong*.

The ASAN Foundation was created to support research, translation and publication in the social sciences and humanities.

Unlike the previous three, the LG Yonam Foundation (Yonam Munhwa Chaedan) focuses on science and technology. The foundation's LG Sangnam Library was Korea's first digital science library.

Evaluation of research

As part of Korea's globalization efforts, researchers are expected to compete with their peers in the rest of the world. Accordingly, the academic evaluation process has become standardized and much more rigorous in recent years, as compared to the past when it was more subjective and informal. Each university has its own standards and guidelines for appointment, promotion and tenure decisions, salary increases, allocation of research funds, etc. However, the system used by the Korea Research Foundation exerts a strong influence on the evaluation systems in all other institutions. Publishing is the single most important criterion in faculty evaluation, and under the current system, where and how often to publish can be more important considerations than what to publish. In other words, the quality of a publication is judged not necessarily by the work itself, but by the medium that carries the work. For domestic publications, only articles published in journals that have met certain KRF quality standards count. There are two tiers of quality ratings: KRF *tungjae* (KRF certified) and KRF *tungjae hubo* (KRF certification candidate). The *tungjae* (certified) journals, the higher of the two tiers, are those that have passed the quality threshold set forth by the KRF. The *hubo* (candidate) journals have not yet reached the minimal threshold but have a good potential to do so within the near future. There are 902 'certified' journals and 533 'candidate' journals, providing publication venues for scholars in the humanities, social sciences and basic sciences. For scientists, publishing in journals covered by the SCI is expected.

Humanists and social scientists contend that the evaluation systems adopted by many institutions are modeled after the American system for science and technology disciplines. They ignore the characteristic differences between the disciplines and thus are not suitable to evaluate research in the humanities. The nature of research in the humanities and social sciences often requires long-term, in-depth studies that can be best embodied in full-length books rather than journal articles. Since their main readership is Korean scholars in Korea, there are few opportunities, let alone reasons, to publish in overseas journals. In contrast, scientists are dealing with issues that are more typically universal in nature and time-sensitive, requiring frequent publications in international journals. Humanities and social science scholars argue that the majority of evaluation systems adopted by universities do not accurately reflect the amount of time and effort to produce each, respectively, and thus have the effect of favoring journal articles over books. This evaluation trend has resulted in a rather unhealthy phenomenon whereby some humanists and social scientists choose to forgo books in favor of shorter journal articles.

Publishing industry

Statistical overview

Before going into specifics about scholarly publishing, an overview of the publishing infrastructure will be useful. As of 2005, the total numbers of registered publishing and printing companies were 24,580 and 7,066, respectively. The number of publishers grew almost tenfold in 20 years, from 2,650 in 1985 to 24,580 in 2005 (Taehak Chulpan Munhwa Hyophoe, 2006). In terms of the number of new publications, it grew from 32,256 titles in 1996 to 43,585 in 2005. Excluding comic books, children's books, learning-aid books and translations, the average number of copies per title was 2,139. The subject ratio of new publications was as follows: literature (18.95 per cent), social sciences (13.25 per cent), technology (8.40 per cent), languages (5.15 per cent), religion (4.66 per cent), arts (3.74 per cent), history (2.98 per cent), science (1.95 per cent), philosophy (1.92 per cent) and general (0.76 per cent). The estimated total market size in 1997, excluding magazines and learning-aid books for students, was US$48 billion. In 2005 it dropped to US$27 billion. One of the contributing factors for this significant reduction must have been the exclusion of textbooks from the depository system, on which the statistics were based (Taehak Chulpan Munhwa Hyophoe, 2006).

The primary form of scholarly publishing is journals, which are mostly published by scholarly associations. Books, on the other hand, are published mostly by commercial publishers and university presses. Various government bodies and research institutes also publish journals, reports, white papers, etc. It is difficult to know what proportion of all publications is scholarly in nature. The closest data come from a survey conducted in 1999 by Hanguk Chulpan Yonguso (Korean Publishing Research Institute). With 819 respondents, it was the most comprehensive study ever conducted on the publishing industry. The results were published in 2000 in a 578-page book entitled *Hanguk Chulpan Sanop Siltae Chosa* (*Survey on the Current State of the Korean Publishing Industry*) (Yun, 2000). According to the study, the largest number of respondents (40.2 per cent) indicated that their main business is books for the general public. The next largest group (38.9 per cent) said their main business is professional/scholarly books. This was followed by publishers whose main business was learning-aid books for students (6.7 per cent), children's books (5 per cent) and general-interest magazines (4.8 per cent). In 1998 the average gross sales for the industry as a whole were US$490,000 per publisher, while the average for the publishers of professional/scholarly books was slightly lower, at US$466,800 per publisher. This translates into combined gross sales of US$148.9 million for all 319 professional/ scholarly book publishers. The average profit for the industry overall was 13 per cent, compared to 14.1 per cent for professional/scholarly book publishers. This higher profit rate for the latter, albeit small, is surprising, but since professional and scholarly books were grouped together, the higher profit rate must come from the professional books, not the scholarly books. It is unfortunate that these categories were not separated. The most profitable sector was children's books (14.8 per cent) and the least profitable was magazines (10.4 per cent). As expected, professional/ scholarly book publishers have a higher rate of steady sellers (9.4 per cent of respondents) than the industry average (8.4 per cent) and a lower rate of bestsellers (3.1 per cent) compared to the industry average (6.7 per cent). Over the course of the companies' histories, seven professional/scholarly publishers reported having produced bestsellers that sold an average of 600,000 copies per title (the industry average for the bestseller category was 1.02 million copies). Twenty-seven professional/scholarly publishers reported having steady sellers that sold an average of 10,300 copies per title over the life of the publication (the industry average for steady sellers was 211,000 copies per title). From this one can see that the thresholds for best and steady sellers for professional/scholarly books are much lower than those for the industry overall.

Journals

According to the 2006 *Chulpan Yongam* (*Korean Publication Yearbook*), there were a total of 4,325 registered serials published more frequently than once a year in 2005, up from 3,779 in 2000 (Taehak Chulpan Munhwa Hyophoe, 2006). While it is unknown how many of these constitute scholarly journals, the number of journals recognized by the KRF for their quality scholarly content is 1,435. These KRF journals form the basis for the Korean Citation Index (KCI), which is freely searchable on the KRF website (www.krf.or.kr/kci). Many of the articles (over 45 per cent) are available in full text from the websites of the associations which publish the journals.

University presses

University presses provide an important publication venue for scholars. The first university press was the Ewha Women's University Press, established in 1949. It was not until the 1960s and 1970s, however, that university presses began proliferating. Today, the Association of Korean University Presses, established in 1982, has 86 members. The association's website reports that 73 members published a total of 18,105 titles, of which 11,653 titles are currently in print (Hanguk Taehak Chulpanbu Hyophoe, 2007). The most prolific academic press, the Seoul National University Press, has published 1,494 titles in its lifetime, followed by the Ewha Women's University Press with 900 published in total, the Yonsei University Press (720) and the Korea University Press (650). These are also the most reputable university presses in Korea. The average publication per press overall was 171 titles.

The most common items published by university presses are books of a scholarly nature written by professors. They also publish textbooks and books for the general public. Considering the fact that universities are home to the largest concentration of scholars, university presses are not as active as they should or might be expected to be. The reason for this phenomenon can be explained by two factors: the abnormal evaluation system of professors as discussed earlier, and the market economy. Since the majority of university press books are for the scholarly community, the market is quite small. Without a support system that guarantees the recovery of expenses, only a handful of university presses can sustain active publishing programs. One support program that benefits university presses (although not exclusively designed for them) is the 'best books' award system. Each year various organizations, most notably the Ministry of Culture and Tourism, select approximately 300–400 'best' scholarly (and other categories of merit) books and distribute them freely to libraries. Books published by university presses are often included in these lists. In 2006 the government spent about US$10.5 million in various publishing support programs, including several categories of 'best books' awards.

Academic research centers

Research centers affiliated with universities also play a role in scholarly communication. Currently there are 2,932 university-affiliated research centers (1,471 in the humanities and social sciences, and 1,461 in sciences, technology and medicine). Many of these centers issue journals. These publications are generally regarded to be of lesser quality compared to the journals published by scholarly associations, because they often lack objective evaluation processes, such as peer review.

Translations

In 2004 approximately 23 per cent of all publications (excluding comics, children's books and learning-aid books) were translations (Taehak Chulpan Munhwa Hyophoe, 2006). Philosophy had the highest rate of translations (43 per cent), followed by religion (30 per cent), literature (30 per cent), general (30 per cent), science (29 per cent), history (24 per cent), social sciences (22 per cent), arts (20 per cent), technology (11 per cent) and languages (10 per cent). The largest numbers of books translated into Korean were originally published in the USA; translations from Japanese constitute the next largest group. Of all the 2004 translations, 48 per cent were works from the USA and 22 per cent were from Japan. In 2005 the overall translation rate decreased from the previous year, as well as the dependency on the USA (44 per cent) and Japan (19 per cent). Translations of Korean works into foreign languages are far fewer in number, although there has been an upward trend. From 1980 to 2005 it is estimated that over 430 Korean works were translated into English, German, French, Spanish, Chinese, Japanese and many other languages.

Electronic publishing

Since Korea's first electronic book was published in 1991 on CD-ROM, electronic publishing grew rather slowly until 1996 when the CD-ROM format began to decline. With the rapidly growing popularity of the internet, electronic books began their migration from CD-ROM to online, starting in 2000. Now the electronic publishing industry has garnered wide acceptance and is well on its way to even further expansion. The past few years' statistics illustrate the growth trend well. In 2000 electronic books, including CD-ROM and online, numbered close to 13,000 titles. The number grew to 45,000 titles in 2003, to more than 100,000 in 2004 and to 220,000 titles in 2005. Sales figures show an even faster growth of more than 1,800 per cent in six years. The total sales of e-books in 2000 were US$3 million; in 2002 they grew to US$12 million; in 2004 to US$25 million; and US$55 million in 2005 (Taehak Chulpan Munhwa Hyophoe, 2006). The Korean Electronic Publishers Association boasts 71 publishers as members.

The majority of e-books are for school libraries – classics, learning aids and recreational titles. In recent years university textbooks have been increasingly taking electronic form. Although scholarly titles constitute only a fraction of the overall publishing industry, e-publishing is surely changing the paradigm of scholarly communication in terms of how information is published, marketed and accessed.

One type of electronic publishing involves the digitization of existing print journals. These e-journals are particularly popular in the library and academic communities because of their many advantages over the corresponding print versions: the availability of entire runs of journals, the ease of access and integrated searching.

Recently, an increasing number of journals are 'born digital' and lack print counterparts. Hakhoe Chongbohwa Saop (the Scholarly Society Automation Project) provides a good example of a born-digital publication system. The goal of this project is to provide a one-stop service for all processes related to running a scholarly society. As part of the project, the Korea Institute of Science and Technology Information (KISTI) developed a system called KISTI-ACOMS (Article Contribution Management System). This system provides automated services for membership management, article submission, peer review, communication of review status, managing submitted articles, online publishing of accepted articles, bibliographic and full-text searching, access to the society's publications and conferencing functions.

Another format that is growing in popularity is printing-on-demand. This method is popular for custom textbooks, research monographs and small runs of academic books.

Libraries

The first formal library education program was established in 1957 at Yonsei University with the help of the Peabody College of Teachers. Unfortunately, during the period from 1960 to 1987 when Korea was ruled by a succession of military dictators, the fledgling field of modern librarianship in Korea had no a chance to mature into a high-level profession. During this time many libraries, run by non-librarians, served merely as quiet study halls. Those who worked in libraries (not necessarily trained librarians) were commonly perceived as rude, ignorant, lazy and incapable bureaucrats. These were the conditions until 1987. Then democratization movements swept the country like wildfires in the late 1980s, helping finally to end the long, autocratic regimes. Along with all other sectors of society, libraries began a reformation process and over time have transformed themselves. By the late 1990s card catalog records had been converted and put online, book stacks had opened up and staff qualifications had improved. Today, academic libraries are highly advanced and dynamic institutions with competent and eager professionals providing sophisticated technologies and services to their students and faculty.

National 'informatization' project

The 1997 financial crisis that forced Korea into an IMF bail-out program was one of the most frightening and painful memories in Korean history. Yet, ironically, it served as perhaps the single most powerful catalyst for advancing scholarly communication and libraries in modern history. Convinced that information technology would help create synergies across industrial sectors and enhance Korea's competitiveness, the government coined the term 'informatization' (meaning a process of creating an advanced information society) and adopted it as a core strategy in its effort to emerge from the turmoil of restructuring its troubled economy. The government reasoned that information technology would simplify work processes and trim surplus labor, and thus accelerate the restructuring process. Over the next few years necessary legislation, policies and infrastructure were put in place, and the government invested heavily in 'informatization', aiming to create an advanced information society. Billions of dollars were spent on digitizing significant holdings of libraries, research institutes, museums and governments, and on the development of discovery tools (metadata) and other databases that many other countries can only dream about. Today, ten years later, Korea is one of the most advanced countries in the world in terms of information technology and digital content, poised to create the world's first 'ubiquitous society'. Physical collections of a single library have become less of an issue now that virtual libraries are becoming a reality in Korea. Korean scholars, as well as the general public, enjoy easy access to a rich array of information and research resources in the comfort of their homes or offices via the internet.

Physical libraries

As of December 2005 Korea had 11,839 libraries altogether, including two large national libraries, 438 college/university libraries and 589 special libraries (affiliated with research institutes, government bodies, for-profit or non-profit organizations) (Hanguk Tosogwan Hyophoe, 2006). The rest were public (514) and school (10,297) libraries. The average holdings of the 438 academic libraries are close to 220,000 volumes per library. The combined holdings of the 589 special libraries are over 13 million volumes. The collection sizes of special libraries are generally small, with average holdings of 15,300 volumes. However, these collections are known for their depth in specialized subjects and/or formats (e.g. multimedia).

National libraries

The two national libraries are the National Library of Korea (NLK) and the National Assembly Library of Korea (NALK). Both play important roles in collecting and preserving materials, in compiling national bibliographies and in leadership. By law, all publications in Korea are deposited into the NLK through a depository system, and it also runs the ISBN and ISSN centers. The NLK serves the general public; the NALK's primary clientele are the legislators and their staff, but the library also serves the general public aged 18 and over. While there is an overlap between the two libraries' collections and services, they try to complement each other by coordinating their activities. The NALK focuses on the social sciences while the NLK concentrates on the humanities.

Bibliographic utilities and tools

The Research Information Service System (RISS) (www.riss4u.net) is the scholarly arm of the Korean Education and Research Information Service (KERIS), a national service organization for education and research programs. Similar to the OCLC, RISS is the largest academic bibliographic utility in Korea. Its databases and services include the union catalog of more than 7.5 million records from 385 academic libraries and 120 special libraries; more than 930,000 articles from more than 4,300 domestic journals (74 per cent of all journals), many of them full text; more than 470,000 full-text dissertations from some 150 universities and 20,000 foreign dissertations on Korea or by Koreans; interlibrary loans/document delivery services; foreign databases, etc. Recently, KERIS announced a new service targeted at overseas libraries called RISS International, which is basically RISS with an English interface. The members of this new fee-based service will be able to download the KOMARC (Korean Machine Readable Catalog) records in the RISS union catalog directly into their local library system in MARC21 format.

The Korea Institute of Science and Technology Information, established in 1962, conducts research on technology, policies and standardization concerning information management and dissemination. KISTI built a supercomputer infrastructure for national R&D programs, constructed the High-Performance Research Network and provides science and technology information database services.

The two national libraries have developed extensive digital content and made this content freely available. The following are among the most popular bibliographic tools.

Mokcha Chongbo (Table of Contents Database) is the index to every item that appears in the tables of contents of the more than 5 million volumes of books or magazines held by the National Library of Korea. This remarkable database is searchable from the NLK's integrated database on the web (www.nl.go.kr).

Chonggi Kanhaengmul Kisa Saegin (Index to Periodical Articles) by the National Assembly Library of Korea is the most comprehensive index to scholarly or otherwise 'high-quality' articles published in Korea since 1910. From 1999 to June 2005 it was published on CD-ROM, but now it is on the web as a searchable database. As of January 2007 some 2.2 million articles had been indexed, of which more than 654,000, mostly in the social sciences, are directly linked to their full-text images as TIFF or PDF files.

Hanguk Paksa mit Soksa Hagwi Nonmun Chong Mongnok (Union Catalog of Korean Dissertations and Theses), also provided by the National

Assembly Library, is the most comprehensive dissertation database in Korea. Of the 1,003,000 bibliographic records for domestic dissertations and theses written since 1945, 507,000 are available in full-text format. The bibliographic records and public domain materials are freely searchable on the NALK's website (www.nanet.go.kr) by title, author, keyword, university and table of contents. Copyrighted materials are, however, accessible only through a licensing agreement between the NALK and other institutions.

There are three citation indexes in Korea, searchable freely on the web: the previously mentioned Korean Citation Index, the Korean Science Citation Index and the Korean Medical Citation Index.

Commercial database services

A handful of companies compete for a share of the scholarly database market. Among them, the following companies are best known.

Korean Studies Information (KSI) was established in 1992. Its web database is called KISS (Korean Studies Information Service System) (kiss.kstudy.com). KSI's most popular product is its Fulltext Online Journals, which contains over 1 million research articles from 3,500 publications covering all subject areas since 1945. Coverage begins with the first issue of publication and continues through to the current issue, with no gaps. Approximately 100,000 items are added each year. Another popular product is Newspaper Archives, providing access to 350,000 pages of the *Choson Ilbo* from the first issue in 1920 to the current date. In 2007 another major newspaper, the *Tonga Ilbo*, will be added. The Printed Books (i.e. digitized) & E-Books (i.e. born digital) database holds 3,000 titles as of May 2007, with more than 100 academic monographs added each month. These databases are available through institutional license agreements only, with IP address authentication. KSI also offers an on-demand publishing and printing service for textbooks, research monographs and small print runs of academic books.

Another important company is Nuri Media (www.nuri.co.kr). Nuri's full-text journal service is called DBPia, and offers 866 journals (631,533 articles) in 11 subject fields. KRPia is a Korean studies database, consisting of many digitized titles of classical works and dictionaries in Korean studies. As with KSI, these databases are available through institutional license agreements only, with IP address authentication. For independent scholars who have no institutional affiliations, Nuri provides a document delivery service in partnership with Kyobo Book Center, the largest bookstore in Korea.

Digital libraries

In addition to the databases already mentioned, various digital libraries are being created to preserve and broaden access to both current and early (pre-1945) Korean imprints. While there have been no systematic nationwide attempts to survey and identify all the surviving older Korean imprints, it is estimated that approximately 3.3 million such items exist throughout the country. Of about 2 million items that have been identified, university libraries hold approximately 1.5 million items, and museums, used bookstores and individual families hold the rest. These titles, along with other important collections, have been selectively digitized, and form an important corpus of national digital libraries. Although the physical items are scattered throughout many institutions, their descriptions and digital images can be searched in integrated databases at any time anywhere in the world, through the following portal websites:

- Korean Knowledge Portal – www.knowledge.go.kr
- National Digital Library – www.dlibrary.go.kr
- Korean History Online – www.koreanhistory.or.kr
- Union Catalog of Korean Classics – www.nl.go.kr/korcis
- Korea National Heritage Online – www.heritage.go.kr.

The magnitude and breadth of these free resources are truly amazing. Additional resources are continuously being added thanks to the Intellectual Resources Preservation Act. Current digitization projects include private and institutional collections sponsored by the Ministry of Information and Communication, and university holdings sponsored by the Ministry of Education and Human Resources. The goal of the latter is to convert the bibliographic records for all early Korean imprints held by universities, and digitize 45,000 volumes of important titles.

Special libraries

Of the many special libraries, the following are noteworthy.

The Korean Social Science Library (www.kssl.or.kr) was established in 1983 by the Esquire Cultural Foundation, a private foundation. In 2003 the library established the Korean Social Survey Data Archive as an added service to social scientists. The archive identifies, collects, preserves and facilitates access to raw data from various social surveys related to Korea.

The Korean Social Sciences Data Center is supported by the Ministry of Education and Human Resources. Its goal is systematically to collect and manage important statistical and survey data. Currently there are 40,000 sets of raw data, which are accessible through RISS.

Resource sharing

As the production of new knowledge is growing exponentially and the new trend of interdisciplinary research requires access to more diverse information than ever before, Korean libraries, whose dependency on foreign knowledge is very high, find it increasingly difficult to meet all their users' needs independently. Scholarly information has become essential for survival in this age of international competition, and yet it has become impossible and too expensive for any single institution to collect everything being published today. Until the Korean financial crisis that started in 1997, most academic libraries had worked largely independently, building their own collections and serving their own users on their campuses. Faced with big budget cuts as a result of the financial crisis and soaring foreign journal subscription costs, university libraries began actively exploring ways to stretch their budgets. As a result, many consortia were formed, with or without the government's backing. Some of them are nationwide in scope, while others operate within certain geographic boundaries. Most of these cooperative programs are not limited to online resources but also include print collections with a document delivery service component. As of 2006, more than 300 libraries in Korea participate in one or more of the over 70 consortia.

KERIS and KISTI provide leadership and oversight for collective purchasing agreements for foreign databases. KERIS focuses on the humanities and social sciences and provides oversight of 92 consortia agreements for 158 libraries. KISTI specializes in science and technology databases. As part of the National Digital Science Library (NDSL) project, KISTI formed the Korean Electronic Site License Initiative (KESLI), which was modeled after NESLI (National Electronic Site Licence Initiative), a similar initiative in the UK. Patrons can submit interlibrary loan (ILL) or document delivery service (DDS) requests directly online through RISS or KISTI. While KERIS is limited to domestic ILL/DDS, the scope of KISTI's NDSL is international. Another major document delivery consortium is the Korea Resource Sharing Alliance (KORSA), operated by the Kwangju Kwahak Kisurwon

(Gwangju Institute of Science and Technology). Unlike KERIS and KISTI, which are government supported, KORSA is a private organization supported entirely by membership, which currently includes 150 university libraries.

Foreign research information centers

Another organized effort involves the creation of regional centers for the purpose of systematically identifying and securing at least one subscription for potentially important foreign journals in a given subject. The first such center, the Electronic and Telecommunication Engineering Database Center, was established at the Kyongbuk National University in 2006 with the financial support of the Ministry of Education and Human Resources. The center subscribes to 838 foreign journals (and the number is growing), and supplies articles nationally through a document delivery system upon request. The plan is to create similar centers for ten other subject categories at ten major research universities.

Korean Collections Consortium of North America

This is a cooperative collection development and resource-sharing consortium in support of Korean studies based in North America. Sponsored by the Korea Foundation, it began in 1991 with six US research universities with significant Korean studies programs. Each member library was given the responsibility of collecting in certain subject areas according to prearranged plans so as to avoid duplication among members. The consortium collections are loaned freely through ILL systems to any scholar in North America, not just to consortium members. The six founding members were the University of California at Berkeley, Columbia University, Harvard University, the University of Hawaii, the University of Southern California and the University of Washington. By 2007 the membership had doubled, and now includes two Canadian institutions. The additional members are the University of British Columbia, the University of California at Los Angeles, the University of Chicago, the University of Michigan, Stanford University and the University of Toronto. These 12 institutions represent the largest Korean studies centers in North America.

dCollections

dCollections is an institutional repository consortium sponsored and facilitated by KERIS, which developed software and provided it to participating universities (currently 60 and growing). In this system, authors submit their works along with descriptive metadata directly to their universities using the software developed by KERIS. The files are converted into the appropriate format and stored in the repository within the university. The metadata and location information for the work are integrated into RISS. In this cooperative program, each participating university collects, catalogs, houses, preserves and disseminates the intellectual output of the institution in digital form. This could include materials such as research journal articles, theses and dissertations. The main objective of dCollections is to provide open access to institutional research by self-archiving it, thereby enhancing scholarly communication while reducing costs.

Copyright

Since intellectual property and copyright issues are relatively new concepts to Koreans, illegal copying was a common practice until recently. Similarly, until 1987, when Korea affiliated with the Universal Copyright Convention (UCC), piracy was also a common phenomenon. After joining the UCC, Korea entered into many major international copyright treaties, including the Berne Convention for the Protection of Literary and Artistic Works in 1996. Since then, Korea has become fully compliant with international copyright conventions and has shed its former negative image of being a pirate country.

Scholars did not pay much attention to the copyright of their journal articles until commercial database companies began reaping profits by digitizing and marketing their published works. Commercial publishers obtain digitization rights from scholarly associations and sell usage licenses for the resulting databases to libraries for profit. In 2005 a graduate student at Daegu University conducted a study on copyright practices of scholarly journals by surveying 166 associations randomly selected from the KRF's scholarly association database (Yi, 2005). The study revealed that, for 29.5 per cent of the journals surveyed, the scholarly associations that published the journals held the copyright. Only 1.2 per cent of those surveyed indicated that both the associations and the authors co-owned the copyright. The majority (69.3 per cent) had no copyright statements, leaving room for copyright disputes. The fact that many of these scholarly articles result from research grants supported by the government or other public funds, as well as the increasing trend of self-archiving and institutional repositories, contribute to the copyright complexities. Dissertations present yet another set of challenges. University libraries routinely seek a release of copyright for dissertations and theses from their graduating students, but they are not always successful. Those dissertations under copyright protection must be managed accordingly.

Korean copyright law was revised in 2003 to reflect better the changing nature of accessing, copying and transmitting copyrighted materials in the digital age. The new revisions were an attempt to strike a balance between conflicting interests – namely the author's right to protect his/her intellectual/artistic creation from exploitation and the users' right to have convenient and affordable access to information. The goal of the government is, on the one hand, to encourage wide access to accelerate the dissemination of information and, on the other, to protect authors so as to induce more intellectual and artistic output. The 2003 revisions incorporated more restrictions applying to libraries than the 2000 revisions, requiring usage fees when a copyrighted work is printed or digitally transmitted beyond the holding library.

Copyright management

In compliance with Article 28 of the Korean Copyright Law, which states that libraries must assess fees for copying and transmitting copyrighted works, Hanguk Poksa Chonsongkwon Kwalli Sento (the Korean Reprographic and Transmission Rights Center, or KRTRC) was established in July 2004 to facilitate the collection and distribution of copyright fees. The KRTRC basically acts as a broker between libraries and copyright owners, thus relieving both of the onerous task of tracking each other down. The libraries and individuals wishing to avail themselves of the KRTRC's services must sign an agreement with the KRTRC. They also need to sign agreements with the individual libraries with which they will have transactions. Once these agreements are in place, users can access the restricted resources via authorized IP addresses. As of May 2007, 611 libraries had signed up for the KRTRC's service, including one overseas library, the University of Southern California in Los Angeles. Libraries have the option of having the usage fees paid by end users or by the library. The fees are extremely inexpensive, as shown in Table 4.1.

Table 4.1 Copyright fees for copying and transmitting library materials

Categories		Printing	Transmission to other libraries (including copying for transmission purposes)
Monographs	For-sale items	0.5 cent per page	2 cents per file
	Not-for-sale items	0.3 cent per page	0
Periodicals	For-sale items	0.5 cent per page	2 cents per file
	Not-for-sale items	0.3 cent per page	0

Not all libraries in Korea welcomed the KRTRC. Those which opposed it maintain that the center is too bureaucratic and imposes an undue burden on individual libraries; in 2004 they formed a new group called Hagwi Nonmun Wonmun Kongdong Iyong Hyobuihoe (Consortium to Share Fulltext Dissertations). Led by the Seoul National University, the group's objective is to share dissertations of member universities through open access and institutional repositories. By May 2007 the membership stood at 161 universities and the database consisted of 220,836 dissertations contributed by 55 universities. However, membership is not open to overseas libraries as of May 2007, pending some legal disputes.

Areas for improvement

The astonishing speed of library development in Korea has not been without its downsides, including the shortage of careful coordination and the uneven quality of catalog records.

Libraries began pooling their resources by forming various consortia – and yet they still have a long way to go. Approximately 50 per cent of all Korean subscriptions to foreign journals are duplicated among many institutions, while certain essential titles are not subscribed to by a single library. Better planning and coordination will help to divide collection responsibilities among libraries so as to ensure wide coverage while reducing duplication and gaps in holdings. Through careful and smart strategic planning, libraries should be able to develop a comprehensive collection as a whole, while promoting specialization and diversification in individual libraries according to their institutional strengths. KERIS and KISTI, the two national organizations that provide leadership in cooperative programs, divide their work by large subject categories, but their efforts often overlap. The same goes for the two national libraries. A more systematic coordination among leadership institutions, as well as among individual libraries, is highly desirable to minimize waste and maximize benefits.

Quality bibliographic records are a prerequisite for effective access to scholarly information. While the RISS database developed by KERIS is a significant accomplishment, the quality of individual records is uneven and needs improvement. Most serial titles lack holdings information, and non-standardized cataloging practices result in the creation of many unnecessary duplicate records. In order for RISS to serve as the truly useful international bibliographic utility it strives to be, the quality of its records must be improved to meet international standards for bibliographic control.

Future trends

One-stop service portals

Korea was preoccupied in the past decade with converting its printed knowledge to digital format. Now the country is pondering how best to process, package and disseminate the information to make it more valuable, accessible and usable. Toward that end, scholarly information in Korea is increasingly disseminated via commercial search engines, such as Empas, Naver, Google and Yahoo. In addition, sophisticated one-stop service portals are being designed and built. One example is the KRF's comprehensive research information management system. At present, researchers must report and submit their research output to both their employers and the KRF. In an attempt to eliminate this unnecessary duplication of effort and to integrate and share disparate information through a network, the KRF is developing a comprehensive database or clearing-house on national research output information, called Kukka Yongu Opchok Tonghap Chongbo Sisutem (National Research Output Information System). When this new system is implemented, it is expected to provide one-stop services for everything related to research in Korea. The system will be networked with other research databases such as patents' databases, the Korean Citation Index, the Science Citation Index etc., which will help to expedite the authentication process.

Open access and institutional repositories

Most domestic journals are published by non-profit scholarly associations, and are supplied to individuals and institutions at inexpensive subscription prices. In that sense, as far as domestic journals are concerned, libraries do not have the subscription crises which affect Western research libraries. Still, open access and institutional repositories are of interest to Korean libraries and scholars for two reasons: Korean scholars depend a great deal on foreign journals and libraries must meet their needs; and the Korean copyright laws require libraries to pay usage fees when copyrighted works in digital format are printed or transmitted. Open access and institutional repositories are thus being actively explored and implemented, as in the aforementioned dCollections project.

Ubiquitous society

As stated before, Korea's ambition is to become the first 'ubiquitous society' in the world. A ubiquitous society suggests 'a world in which information can be accessed from anywhere, at any time, by anyone and anything'. In the future, ubiquitous networks will extend beyond person-to-person and person-to-object connectivity, uniting everyday things in one huge communications network. Compared to the business sector, which has embraced this goal enthusiastically, academia has been slow in adopting cutting-edge technologies that make a ubiquitous society possible. In recent years, however, new technologies are increasingly finding their way to university campuses. Students can access many academic services using real-time transactions to register, add/drop courses, send and receive e-mail etc. through their mobile phones or PDA. Recent examples of such transformations include Kyemyong University, Pusan National University and Songgyungwan University. Many libraries are replacing the barcodes in their books and on library cards with radio-frequency identification tags.

In reflecting upon the degree of Korea's transformation over the past few decades, it is difficult to imagine what it will be like in the coming years. One thing is sure: the resilience and passion for learning that sustained Korea's cultural heritage for millennia will continue to guide the Korean people. What form and shape this will take in this fast-paced age, only time will tell.

Future challenges

In concluding this chapter, it is sad that this is only half the picture. Very little is known about North Korea, the other half of the Korean peninsula, and its people, beyond the fact that the communist government tightly controls everything there, including academic endeavors of scholars. One can imagine what the country is like when North Korean encyclopedias and dictionaries begin with the name of their 'Dear Leader', the president and chairman of the Communist Party, not the first letter of the alphabet. When the two Koreas are reunited, South Korean scholars will finally have access to the missing pieces which will provide a complete picture for their scholarly pursuits, and vice versa. The present authors only hope that they will have an opportunity to write a whole chapter in their lifetime.

5

Scholarly communication in Taiwan

Jingfeng Xia and Mei-Mei Wu

Taiwan is an island in East Asia, off the south-eastern coast of mainland China, and was first inhabited by humans as early as 30,000 years ago. In the past 400 years Taiwan has been through different historical stages, including European colonization, the reign of the Jheng family, imperial Chinese rule, Japanese colonization and the Republic of China (ROC). Scholarly communication is not isolated from the development of education, particularly higher education, publishing and libraries of all kinds, which are all dependent on public policy. Under imperial rule, scholarship followed Confucian tradition and was facilitated by an imperial examination system. The traditional education was through an academy of classical learning and home schooling with private tutors. After the Japanese invaded and occupied the island in 1894, the Western type of higher education was introduced. However, the purpose of higher education during that period was for colonial economic development and had nothing to do with the promotion of scholarship.

It was not until after the end of the Second World War in 1945, and when the ROC retreated from mainland China and relocated in Taiwan in 1949, that a real system of higher education was developed and scholarship in Taiwan began to be established. Since then the government has focused on the development of education as a necessary step in the advancement of democracy and the economy. At the same time, other scholarly pursuits such as publishing and information circulation through libraries and professional activities were also developed in a systematic way. In the past decade Taiwan has joined the venture of digital communication and has made great contributions to the reshaping of new scholarly communications, both locally and internationally. This chapter briefly discusses the achievements and issues related to scholarly activities using recent data and current status.

Higher education

Higher education in Taiwan, though with a short history, has experienced a rapid development. Before the ROC, the Taipei Imperial University was for many years the only higher educational institution. Within a period of two decades after the ROC moved to Taiwan, more than 30 universities and colleges were founded with a total annual enrollment of around 80,000 students. These figures do not include junior colleges, which outnumbered public institutions. Compared to one university and three colleges in the early 1950s, this quick growth was concurrent with development in all other areas that a newly established government needs for ordinary operations. It also reflected the demand of society for qualified manpower to participate in the building of economic modernization and the continuation of cultural tradition. By the new millennium, institutions of higher education had increased to more than 150, with student enrollment reaching 1 million.

The government adjusts the direction of higher education through its policies as well as by direct financial support to universities and colleges. In the past three decades there have been several leaps, particularly between 1986 and 1995 when the number of universities and colleges jumped from 28 to 60. Another two leaps were in 1998–1999 and 2005–2006. The following figures indicate the results of government interventions in balancing public and private institutions and redistributing the student population for societal needs: the number of junior colleges was reduced from 53 to 17 with a decrease of students from 452,346 to 180,886, and the number of colleges and universities was increased from 84 to 145, with an expansion of student enrollment from 463,575 to 1,115,672. The number of masters' students also increased from 43,025 to 149,493, and the number of doctoral students rose from 10,845 to 27,531.

Certainly, the rapid growth has brought prosperity to the academic community and contributed to manufacturing industry. Yet, on the other hand, the growth rate has been considered to be too fast and has caused some problems in higher education. When the number of junior colleges increased rapidly in the late 1960s, there were so many of their graduates that society found it difficult to use all of them, resulting in an increased unemployment rate. At the same time, the quality of education at these junior colleges was widely questioned when a paradigm shift of economic models from manufacturing to information industry took place. The adjustment process reflected these issues. For universities, a recent fast growth in number raises concern about their future sustainability, since the government is the only source of financial support. They may need to develop plans to deal with potential budget cuts, even given the fact that public funding in recent years has amplified. However, the problem of budget constraints in higher education is also common in other countries.

In Taiwan, higher education is composed of universities, colleges and junior colleges. Much like higher education in other countries, universities are mostly academic organizations designed for research and educating advanced students, while colleges are more specialized and may grant degrees above the bachelor level, although most only have undergraduate students. Some universities and colleges are public institutions because of their government funding. In contrast, many junior colleges are open to investment by private resources and may depend for survival on the market. Because of this, junior colleges have largely developed curricula tailored to the needs of economic development, and focus primarily on vocational training for special professions such as the sciences and engineering. Junior colleges are further divided into two-year colleges and five-year colleges, the former outnumbering the latter, and both offering an associate degree or its equivalent. There has been a tendency in the past few years for junior colleges to be converted into institutes of technology.

College admission rates differ between universities/colleges (more than half of the applicant pool) and junior colleges (less than half). Higher scores in a national university entrance examination are always required to get into the most prestigious universities. Over the years admission rates have been raised to reflect an ever-growing population on the island. This has brought up the issue of the teacher-to-student ratio, because the increase in faculty can never catch up with the increase in students. The unemployment rate has also risen, although it has always been less than 4 per cent, which is as low as in many developed countries. Access to higher education, especially private institutions, is very expensive for students. Tuition and fees in private schools can be three to four times as much as in public schools. However, higher educational costs in both private and public sectors have been diminishing over the past decades, making education more affordable for the average household.

Although universities in Taiwan are rooted in the synthesis of Japanese and traditional Chinese educational systems, their organizational structures are more like those of the USA. The management chain of a university runs from president to dean to department chair.

Academically, lecturers and assistant, associate and full professors take responsibility for teaching students and carrying out research projects. Many faculty members at top research universities maintain close collaborations with scholars in independent research institutions such as the Academia Sinica. The latter are sometimes invited to be adjunct professors at universities. In terms of the research quality, it is traditionally considered that public universities are more prestigious than private ones. Among all universities, private and public, the National Taiwan University, National Tsing Hua University, National Cheng Kung University and National Chiao Tung University are most highly regarded by continuous university assessments based on faculty productivity, such as research projects and publications. Although this quantitative approach to university ranking has been criticized by many humanities scholars, it is still practiced regularly.

Faculty are evaluated for performance in their teaching and research, the latter of which is usually emphasized based on the amount of grant funding and the number of publications. The productivity of scholars is measured by citations of their work in the SCI, SSCI, SCIE, A&HCI, EI and TSSCI. According to the National Science Council, the total number of research papers published in 2001 was 13,490 (National Science Council of Taiwan, 2003). This number was divided by the number of full-time faculty to yield an annual average productivity of 0.21, which is unfortunately lower than in many other developed countries. The major areas of publications identified were medicine and natural sciences, comprising 35.7 per cent and 32.0 per cent respectively. This may reflect the allocation of major research grants by the government in recent years.

Almost all the major universities in Taiwan offer some kind of incentive to encourage scholarly publishing. The incentive policies include providing grants for research, awarding cutting-edge projects and supporting attending professional conferences. For example, the National Taiwan University and National Chengchi University have funded scholarly journals to publish faculty research. The National Chengchi University and National Tsing Hua University have offered research awards for research excellence at various levels. The National Cheng Kung University, National Chiao Tung University and National Sun Yat Sen University have sponsored their faculty to attend international conferences and publish monographs. Other universities have offered reduced teaching hours so that faculty can concentrate on research projects.

Publishing

Brief history

The publishing industry in Taiwan has experienced several major changes as the result of political transformations and social reforms throughout history. During the Japanese colonization (1895–1945), publishing was under the authority of the Japanese, who undertook a plan to reorient the society into a Japanese tradition. The language of formal education at all levels was Japanese. Chinese-language publications were very rare, and traditional Chinese scholarly activities were completely abandoned. There was some private printing in romanized Taiwanese, mostly religious materials. However, because of their private nature, no archival documents recording these have been found.

When Taiwan was handed over to the ROC in the late 1940s, the central government took two major steps to regenerate scholarly communication. First, it tried to replace the Japanese system with a new one that strongly emphasized ethnic identity, to eradicate memories of foreign rule. Second, learning from the failure of the communists in mainland China, it tried to tighten control of people's thoughts to avoid any possible threat by the citizens to government rule. Anti-mainland China propaganda was developed and soon spread all over the island. This firm control was most visible in the publishing industry, within which political censorship was sternly imposed.

From the beginning of the ROC regime, the imposition of martial law in publishing was based on two legal sources, the Law of Publications and the Measure of Publications Control Under Martial Law, and enforced by several government agencies – the Cultural Committee, the Taiwan Garrison Command and the Government Information Office. The implementation of the laws was so strict that authors could be harassed, detained or even jailed. All types of media, including books and journals, were subject to censorship. A healthy scholarly communication system could not survive under such strong ideological control.

The year 1987 witnessed a political transformation from a repressed environment to a democratic society, symbolized by the government's announcement of the end of martial law, and thus the censorship of publications. The decades-long restriction was followed by instant flourishing in publishing as well as in other scholarly areas. People were able to express their ideas freely; books could be published regardless of their political orientation; and publications and scholarly opinions from mainland China became available. Development of the economy from the mid-1960s made the rapid expansion of scholarly communication possible, and played a key role in redirecting its development. The government also provided support to assist scholarly conduct through incentive policies, e.g. encouraging a peer-review process in scholarly journals, and sponsorship for individual projects, e.g. publishing citation index databases to enhance tracing scholarly output. The Taiwan Social Science Citation Index is one such project, and includes the Citation Index, Journal Citation Report and Journal List Options.

Since the mid-1990s the advancement of ICT has brought an electronic revolution to scholarly publishing in Taiwan. Electronic books and journals appeared, and then became more prevalent in disseminating information and research outcomes, while other forms of electronic publications such as databases have also become widely available. The internet has made communication more efficient.

Monographs

If 'diversity' characterizes the condition of the current publishing industry, 'prosperity' best describes how fast the development of the industry has been in the past two decades. Official statistics show that the number of new book titles was only 4,565 in 1980. It quickly rose to 16,156 in 1990, 34,533 in 2000 and 41,966 titles produced by 8,357 publishers in 2002, rising almost tenfold in 25 years (Government Information Office ROC, 2006). The increased number of publications reflects an increased number of publishers. When the government first lifted its censorship in the late 1980s, there were over 3,000 publishers of varied types supporting the need of readers for both scholarly and popular books. The number of publishers has increased steadily since then: at present there are more than 8,000 publishing houses.

This surge in publication and publisher numbers has brought strong competition to the industry. For those publishers that produce scholarly books, high profitability has never been their ultimate goal. They mostly work to support the scholarly community. For those publishers that provide books for general readers, financial return is their major objective. The strong competition has created two extreme ends of the market – on the one hand, some popular books have been widely published and traded, but on the other hand many titles can only be published in small quantities. This situation forced many publishers to make their business incorporated. Business merging has become the trend, to enable companies to raise sufficient capital and avoid unnecessary management waste, ensuring effectiveness and efficiency in their operation and competition. TOM.COM, a Hong Kong-based internet company, is one of the business giants that have moved into Taiwan's print media sector and purchased many small and medium-sized publishing houses to build an international enterprise. Under pressure from such giants, numerous small publishers have had to develop their own survival strategies and target specialized groups of readers.

In past decades the publishing of picture books and big-name translations brought enormous success to the publishing industry. The success was lately extended to mainland China's market, where famous pictorial series dominated the publications imported from Taiwan. Most of the pictorial books use illustrations and brief captions to describe historical stories, and are one of the best sources from which children learn Chinese culture and history.

Monographs are major publications in support of scholarly activities, such as textbooks for college students. Unlike other scholarly books, textbooks are profitable and published by both commercial and academic publishers. The market for academic textbooks and reference books is estimated to be worth more than $10 billion, and an increasing population of university students will enlarge this market. With such an opportunity for profit, textbooks, particularly foreign textbooks, became the victim of piracy and illegal publishing in the 1980s. Illegal duplicates gradually disappeared in the 1990s because of the implementation of copyright law.

Scholarly work from outside the island has become more and more visible, and is important to the development of scholarly communication. Scholarly exchange between the two sides of the Strait (Taiwan and mainland China) is now normal practice. Taiwanese researchers are interested in introducing books from the mainland on topics of cultural heritage, including archaeology, history, philosophy, translations of Western classics and the like. Language in the publications is not a barrier. At the same time, Western books are also in great demand, particularly those with new theories and methods outside the humanities and social sciences. Translated books occupy a considerable proportion of the publication market.

There are different models of scholarly monograph publishing. Commercial publishers, in addition to printing books for general readers, supply some selected scholarly titles. Government-supported publishers, such as Kuo Li Bian Yi Guan (National Institute for Compilation and Translation), work on some national projects and the translation of academic publications in foreign languages with financial support from the government. Specialized academic publishers function to disseminate research work for academia. University presses are an example of the latter publishers.

University presses

Although advocated and proposed earlier, it was not until the 1990s that most university presses appeared. Founded by universities, these presses are under the administration of their sponsors to support teaching and research for the university community and spread scientific knowledge to the public. A recent survey found a total of 102 presses established by 150 higher education institutions (Chiu and Liu, 2003). They vary in size, publishing mission and even English name.

Most public university presses are financially supported by their founding institutions and are designed to serve a particular university. Their publications are generally in the fields of the humanities and social sciences. In practice, these presses are curbed in development by their management models and market plans, because the founding institution of a public university press is its sole customer. Private university presses are more flexible in management and find it easier to reorient their development to meet the needs of the changing market. Recently, both public and private university presses have developed more ambitious plans to enhance the prestige of their universities by introducing high-quality work by their faculty to the international community. More books in the sciences, technology and medicine are being published under these plans.

The publications by university presses have different formats, varying from printed books and journals to electronic versions of research data and results. More than half the presses have been assigned the task of producing academic books and text references. A similar number also manage the publication of journals or bulletins, the former of which are research-oriented while the latter are used as newsletters to publicize university events. In recent years producing electronic journals has become more popular. However, because of limited financial resources for these presses, e-publications are only a small portion of the overall electronic undertaking. The quality of university press publications is controlled by a peer-review process. An editorial committee composed of internal and external experts functions in evaluating publication drafts, either invited by the committee or submitted by individual authors.

University presses have an advantage in supporting academia through their close relationship to academic units. Compared to commercial publishers, they have explicit goals of serving the needs of scholars in higher education. On the other hand, they have a disadvantage when trying to expand business because of their inflexibility in management, including personnel, budgets and distribution channels. It is the job of these publishers to work with university-level administrators to make more effective and efficient plans for further development.

Journals

Scholarly journals are mainly published by academic institutions and professional associations. The Index to Chinese Periodical Literature compiled by the National Central Library covers 4,000-plus journal titles selected from a group of 12,860 journals. Another database – Chinese Electronic Periodical Services – covers 3,445 journal titles. There are 4,825 periodicals produced by commercial publishers, but most academic journals are published by academic societies. There are 4,827 literary and cultural associations, according to statistics from the Ministry of the Interior (2006). In the field of library and information science, a total of 44 journals are published. Most of them are available online with an open source license (Library Association of the Republic of China (Taiwan) and National Central Library, 2007: 60–2).

A peer-review process controls the quality of journal articles. Reviewers are either members of the editorial board of a journal or experts in a given field invited by the chief editor. Chief editors, mostly scholars, take the responsibility of organizing the content of journals and monitoring the submissions. This publishing system is very similar to that of the West.

In most scholarly journals it is common for articles written in Chinese and English to appear in the same issue. Not only do overseas authors contribute English articles to the journals, but many native scholars also do so. Although Chinese is the official language of Taiwan, most scholars and students can read and write English. This is the result of a long preference among college students for studying abroad. From the 1960s, gaining an international degree, particularly in the USA, Japan and Europe, has been normal for those who pursue advanced studies. While in the first two decades the majority of graduates sought career development in the West, since the 1980s more and more graduates have chosen to return to Taiwan with an advanced degree because of the rapid economic growth and increased job opportunities. These graduates now constitute the core of the scholarly team in almost every academic discipline.

The distribution of publications

In general, the distribution channels deal more with books than journals and electronic publications. Distribution is one of the steps making the scholarly communication cycle possible – from original scholarly ideas to production of research results, distribution of published items and consumption of publications. The distribution is undertaken by wholesalers and retailers, which serve as necessary intermediaries connecting publishers to readers. An efficient channel of distribution ensures the success of the publishing industry.

Book distribution in Taiwan is characterized by strong competition between related businesses. Unlike the publishing industry, where several giants monopolize the field to a certain extent, a variety of small to medium-sized wholesale companies and bookstores dominate the distribution landscape. Book retailers are relatively more active than wholesalers: the latter have not been operating very successfully in Taiwan's market. The retailers are grouped into two types: chain stores and individual businesses. Chain bookstores have advantages over individual shops in the size and style of their operation, being able to provide diverse products through more efficient routes to market. Individual bookstores underscore specialties and serve particular groups.

Both wholesalers and retailers have faced increased challenges from the advances in information technologies, particularly the digital movement and the internet. Online orders through the new form of virtual bookstores like Amazon.com have threatened the survival of traditional book distributors. Further challenges came from mainland China when it joined the WTO and opened its book trading market to Chinese-language publishing regions. The cheap book prices on the mainland force Taiwanese businesses to cut costs. Moreover, challenges come from international investment in publication distribution in Taiwan, mainly from Hong Kong and Singapore.

Most wholesalers and retailers take these challenges as opportunities to adjust their ability to compete and maximize their profitability by developing strategies to adapt to the environment. One strategy is to reduce distribution channels so as to lower operational costs. In 2003 an experimental distribution method was created between some chain bookstores and publishers that aimed to eliminate the intermediate wholesalers. Under this contract, the chain bookstores function as display space where publishers can shelve their books for three months. It is not until these newly shelved books are sold that real transactions between the two businesses start. This experiment is good for both ends of the distribution chain – bookstores will be able to reduce their cash investments, and publishers become aware of market requirements by having direct contact with readers.

Another strategy is to build up partnerships with publishers, wholesalers and retailers in mainland China. It is obvious that China has the largest group of readers and is a big market for bookselling. Although lacking the advantage of competitive prices, Taiwanese businesses can benefit from the high quality of their publications and unique topics. In the past, successful businesses have gained through cooperating with their mainland colleagues.

Furthermore, bookstores make great efforts to gain market share by diversifying their business models. Much as Starbucks has successfully moved into libraries in the USA, some Taiwanese chain bookstores enter into partnerships with public services in an effort to make themselves accessible and convenient to a broader group of readers. It may be practical to open a bookstore in a hospital, a theater, a supermarket or any other place where people visit and stay. Such innovative ideas by the Taiwanese may make the channels of publication distribution dynamic and flourishing. It is, of course, still too early to evaluate the pros and cons of this new distribution model.

Book fairs provide an excellent platform for industry professionals to get together and exchange information and ideas. Recently, a Greater Chinese publishing market has been formed to facilitate book exchanges between Taiwan, China, Hong Kong and many other countries and regions interested in Chinese publications. Though not as big as the Beijing Book Fair, the Taipei International Book Exhibition (TIBE), supervised by the Government Information Office, has a longer history and more transparent operation; and after 15 years of operation it has become a strong regional player in the network. Each year thousands of new book titles are brought to the event. Publishers, dealers, authors and book hunters are now not limited to those looking for Chinese materials; many come from non-Chinese communities, such as some Arabic countries.

Libraries

Libraries have successfully functioned to assist academic research, sponsor educational activities, preserve scientific data and findings and provide services for people to access their collection resources. The development of libraries in Taiwan has run parallel with the economic growth since the mid-1960s and reached its peak in the 1980s. In 2006 a total of 5,401 libraries were recorded in official documents, including one national library, 663 public libraries, 173 academic libraries, 498 senior high school libraries, 736 junior high school libraries, 2,650 elementary school libraries and 680 special libraries (Library Association of the Republic of China (Taiwan) and National Central Library, 2007: 49). In recent decades there has been a steady increase not only in the number of libraries but also in collection size, space and circulation.

Since the 1990s, Taiwan's libraries have maintained a close relationship with libraries in mainland China. A wide array of professional activities have enhanced understanding on both sides of the Strait of the achievements and issues in library management and librarianship. In 1993 and 1994 two meetings about China-Taiwan libraries and information services were organized for library professionals to exchange ideas and design future development. Since then the meetings have become regular, and are held every other year in different locations and by different hosts. Libraries across the Strait have also conducted other types of collaborative projects, and benefited much from contact with each other.

Recently, libraries in Taiwan have faced the dilemma of balancing sharp decreases in budget and dramatic increases in publication price, resulting in a shortage of personnel and decreased collection acquisitions. The introduction of digital libraries has brought new challenges. Also, Taiwan's libraries need to reorganize their infrastructure in order to optimize their services and work closer with both the scholarly community and the general public. It is the task of all libraries to maintain the uniqueness of their collections and services, and at the same time join the efforts of libraries all over the world for standardization and globalization.

National Central Library

The National Central Library (NCL) was founded in 1933 in Nanjing, China, and followed the ROC government to Taiwan in 1949.

According to the NCL, its functions include conducting library-related research and development, supporting the growth of domestic libraries and promoting cultural activities to extend society's educational capabilities. As the only national library, the NCL has played a pivotal role in the construction of the profession and has led the general development of libraries in Taiwan. For example, it pioneered the building of digital projects and initiated an online national thesis database as early as 1997. Later the NCL launched a series of digital libraries, including Taiwan Memory, Taiwan Info and Window on Taiwan, to preserve the Chinese cultural heritage and make its unique collections accessible to a broader audience.

According to its statistics, by the end of 2006 the total collection of the NCL encompassed more than 3.3 million items, including roughly 2.3 million books (with approximately 259,000 rare books and some special collections), more than 21,000 journal titles and 400 newspapers, 950,000 non-print materials and 199 kinds of CD-ROM and online database resources (Library Association of the Republic of China (Taiwan) and National Central Library, 2007: 7–8).

The NCL took over the responsibility of managing Taiwan's ISBN system in 1988, and assigned its first ISBN in the following year. Since then, the number of publishers adopting the ISBN system has climbed from 195 to around 13,258 in August 2005. Nowadays 97 per cent of all Taiwanese domestic publishers apply for ISBNs and carry the barcode. The library has been actively working with the ISBN, ISSN, ISRC and CIP systems, with the intention of promoting overseas sales of domestic publications as well as protecting cataloging manpower in all libraries.

Academic libraries

Academic libraries in Taiwan have served the missions of their founding institutions well in supporting learning, teaching and research. The nature of a higher educational institution determines the direction of its library development – comprehensive or specialist. However, all academic libraries have in recent decades faced the challenge of incorporating new technologies into library services. Integrated library automation, appearing in the late 1970s, widespread in the 1980s and continuously improved since then, has built a system in which the sharing of resources across academic libraries is possible.

The internet has brought academic libraries to a new stage of development in the last decade. New forms of library resources include online journal databases, digital libraries, electronic dissertations, etc. Libraries have worked with a variety of information providers, such as publishers (e.g. Elsevier), database suppliers (e.g. EBSCO) and professional associations (e.g. the AMS), to obtain access to scientific journals online. At the same time, libraries have run either independent or collaborative projects to localize electronic resources. Examples of such projects include EdD Online by the National Taiwan Normal University Library for online educational documents, and the eThesys system by the National Sun Yat Sen University Library for theses and dissertations. Almost all academic libraries have also made efforts to build their digital resources, aiming to bring their unique collections to the internet.

Unlike university libraries, libraries of vocational colleges and technology institutes have faced a series of problems in their development. Since the 1990s such types of higher educational institutions have steadily increased in number, but their libraries have not been able to keep up. The major problems include a shortage of trained librarians, library spaces, funding sources, collection numbers and physical facilities. These libraries have not been able to provide necessary support to meet the needs of teaching and research in their host institutions. It is the task of the government to make relevant policies, and of the institutions to reallocate adequate funding, to normalize the development of these libraries in the future.

Public libraries

Public libraries are administered at several different levels – national, municipal, county/city, town/district and special public libraries. The number of public libraries has increased from 439 in 1991 to 687 in 2007. The current size of the collections in all public libraries totals more than 23 million titles. On average a library can serve 35,550 residents, a figure that can meet IFLA criteria but is much lower than in many developed countries. In the past decade, the issue of professional guidelines by the government has helped regulate the operation of public libraries.

Many public libraries have done a great job integrating themselves into the services of local communities. By automating online catalogs to facilitate easy access to library resources and designing user-friendly environments to attract readers from different backgrounds, these libraries have made learning and research a pleasant experience. But public libraries also face problems in shortages of funding and trained professionals, and the imbalance of library geographic distribution. Libraries are clustered in urban centers and are scarce in the rural and mountainous areas. Hopefully, the government will pay more attention to the development of public libraries so that they will be able to provide wider and better services to citizens.

School libraries

School libraries are those operated by high schools and vocational high schools (497), middle schools (723) and elementary schools (2,646). The Ministry of Education set out a series of policies to guide the development of these libraries and allocate funding to support their operations. Teachers, students and parents have worked together to make libraries part of the educational resources. Although elementary schools have the most libraries, libraries of high schools and vocational high schools have provided better collections and services. These libraries have attempted to add value by focusing on assisting high school students in preparation for the national university entrance examinations, and opening their doors to local communities. Currently as many as 76 per cent of high school libraries are open to their communities, and others have a policy or plan to do so.

Special libraries

In terms of the size of collections and number of personnel, special libraries cannot be compared to academic and public libraries because of their limited funding. This does not, however, mean that special libraries do not play an important role in supporting the special needs of varied organizations. On the contrary, some special libraries provide exceptional services to their patrons. They function broadly in serving government agencies, research organizations, non-profit organizations, military units, private companies, hospitals, religious groups, professional associations and the like. In the past decade, the fastest-growing types of special library were those for hospitals and religious groups. Some special libraries are called information centers, and deliver copious information in response to users' requests. Unlike other types of libraries, there is a lack of government policies and professional guidelines to standardize the management of special libraries, leaving them self-structured and diverse.

Science and technology development

Apart from playing a key role in directing science and technology policies, the government also functions in supporting the undertaking of upstream, midstream and downstream studies. Upstream research includes basic research projects conducted by the Academia Sinica and colleges/universities under the Ministry of Education. Midstream research mainly consists of applied research and experimental development conducted by the research units of government agencies under the Executive Yuan, the R&D (research and development) departments of state-run businesses and specially commissioned non-profit research institutions. Downstream research consists of experimental development and commercialization as conducted by private enterprises. The government sector, including the Academia Sinica, encourages more basic and applied research so downstream research has been decreasing over time. Both the higher education and business sectors are also active in basic and applied research activities, although private non-profit organizations conduct only a small part of R&D in Taiwan.

The Academia Sinica is the major governmental research institute, and the National Science Council (NSC) under the Executive Yuan is the major government agency for making policies for scientific development and scholarship. The NSC's Information Center offers 11 bibliographic databases, including technical reports, journal articles, conference papers, etc. Major research institutions and organizations supported by the NSC are discussed below.

National Applied Research Laboratories

As a non-profit organization founded by the NSC in June 2003, the National Applied Research Laboratories (NARL) has consolidated nine national laboratories into an independent non-profit institute – the National Nano Device Laboratory, National Laboratory Animal Center, National Space Organization, National Center for Research on Earthquake Engineering, National Center for High-Performance Computing, National Chip Implementation Center, Science and Technology Policy Research and Information Center, Instrument Technology Research Center and Preparatory Office of National Center for Ocean Research. The NARL's goals are to create and manage a large-scale R&D facility for academic research, and cultivate the necessary manpower in various advanced fields. The NARL also supports diverse academic studies and promotes the vertical integration of the nation's technology development system through conducting applied research to connect fundamental research to product development.

Industrial Technology Research Institute

Established by the Ministry of Economic Affairs in 1973, this institute is one of the largest non-profit research organizations in Taiwan. With a total staff of 5,442 by the end of 2005, it receives about half its funding from the government and half from industry. It strives to help businesses develop products and manufacturing techniques, and has played an essential role in the transformation of the economy from an agriculture-based model to an industrial one. It serves as the technical center for industry and is an informal part of the government's industrial policies in Taiwan. With its broad research scope and close industrial ties, the institute has become active in the global industrial R&D community.

Institute for Information Industry

This institute was founded in 1979 with the purpose of increasing Taiwan's global competitiveness by developing information technology infrastructure and industry. It has been a key contributor of technology to the ICT industry and helped promote the adoption of ICT in both public and private sectors. The institute has served in a number of capacities, such as functioning as a think-tank on ICT policy, offering innovative R&D and interoperability standards for the industry, encouraging ICT applications and narrowing the digital divide. It promotes the progress of the e-Taiwan project and intends to transform the island into one of Asia's leading regions for digital development. With four major research branches, the institute specializes in information engineering, network and multimedia, advanced e-commerce and digital education. Since 1999 it has trained over 300,000 IT professionals and filed more than 100 patent applications annually.

Digital communications

Digital collections

Taiwan has two advantages in developing digital projects to promote research activities and preserve scientific information. First, it has developed into the fourth-largest computer hardware manufacturer in the world; and second, its internet usage has been among the highest globally. The government adopted workable digital plans as early as the 1990s. Since then numerous digital libraries have been implemented, and various types of research organizations have participated in the efforts. Both the scholarly community and broader society have benefited from digitization of academic research and cultural heritage. The following paragraphs do not give a full history of digital project development, but highlight some major achievements in the process.

Over the years, digital projects were started at different levels in varied forms. At the national level, the government launched the e-Taiwan (electronic) and m-Taiwan (mobile) projects to augment economic competitiveness and maintain cultural traditions. The m-Taiwan plan is expected to widen the accessibility of information by reinforcing the wireless networks, integrating mobile phone networks, building optical fiber backbones and executing the Integrated Beyond 3rd Generation (iB3G) Double Network Integration Plan. The e-Taiwan project comprises a series of initiatives and is represented by two major programs – the National Digital Archives Program (NDAP) and the National Science & Technology for e-Learning Program (ELNP).

The NDAP is a five-year program started in 2002. To preserve national cultural collections and promote research, education and lifelong learning, the program coordinates digital content available through leading museums, archives, libraries, research institutions and other major organizational content holders in Taiwan. The ELNP's work aims at creating a high-quality e-learning environment as an integral part of the national efforts to lead Taiwan into a knowledge-based economy. The program involves close cooperation among the government, industry and academia in order to facilitate e-learning in three dimensions – social, industry and research – and bring the pleasures of learning to the public.

At the consortium level, individual organizations have worked together to build common digital projects so as to save resources and share information. The Consortium on Core Electronic Resources in Taiwan (CONCERT) was initiated by the NSC in 1998. It combines different models of information acquisition to provide access to scientific data in support of academia. Most of the data available through CONCERT come from foreign commercial databases, and are obtained by acquiring a national academic license and a consortial license.

The Consortium of Wiley International Serials (CONWIS) consists of five universities and colleges that share their subscribed Wiley electronic journals to lower library costs. In the early stage of the consortium subscriptions were not organized well, resulting in the duplication of electronic content among the members. In 2002 the National Taiwan University Library started to coordinate the contributions of each participating library and optimize the allocations of the resources within the consortium.

The Taiwan EBook Net (TEBNET), founded in 2001, is an e-book consortium. Its purpose is to offer as many volumes of online books published around the world as possible. By reducing the costs of purchasing e-books and increasing e-collections from academic libraries through collaborative development, TEBNET now has 38 institutional members: 22 research universities (13 public and nine private) and 16 polytechnic universities and colleges. It has collected more than 11,000 e-book titles for its members to open and download.

Another consortium, the Digital Dissertation Consortium, was established in 2001 to access degree work at higher educational institutions. It was advocated by the Academia Sinica and signed up to by more than 20 research universities and major libraries. This online resource is based on subscription to the ProQuest databases in North America. About 60 academic libraries are members of the consortium, and 20,225 theses were accommodated for free access by the end of 2003.

At the organizational level, all types of research institutions – universities, libraries, museums, etc. – and private companies, such as commercial publishers, have developed their own digital projects. Their digitized materials may include electronic journals, books, museum collections and other types of databases. Among them, the earliest digital collections include the National Palace Digital Museum and the NSC's Digital Museum Program in the late 1990s. 'Uniqueness' is the characteristic of such independent digital collections. However, the consortium model seems to have been more popular in practice because of the concern about the high costs of subscription, digitization and preservation.

E-journal databases in Taiwan

The different types of consortia mentioned above have been organized to share research information, mainly electronic journal articles. The resources shared are subscription-based, available through commercial providers in developed countries such as EBSCO and ProQuest, and are in English. There is a need to bring all journal articles written in Chinese and published in Taiwan to the web for scholars to access free of charge.

This requires the digitization of such journals and the maintenance of an online database to contain the digitized articles.

There are three major directories of journals published in Taiwan: the *Chinese Periodicals Directory* (PerioGuide), the *Index to Chinese Periodical Literature* (PerioPath) and the *Current Content of Chinese Periodicals* (PerioTOC). As of 2000, more than 2,700 journal titles were recorded in PerioPath. The number is larger today.

At the turn of the new millennium the Taiwan Academic Network (TANet) project was initiated to digitize and preserve Taiwan's journal articles. Based on the PerioGuide, 892 journals were selected and their articles were made accessible, in full text and abstract, to the public through the internet. This database contains journals in applied sciences, particularly medicine, engineering and business management, and social sciences, mainly education and economics. At the first stage of development, not all journals listed in the database were available online. The online-accessible journals had limited coverage in terms of articles being digitized: most only went back ten years. The database was organized poorly, lacking necessary indexes and abstracts to make searching easy. Also, file formats were not standardized and included MS Word, HTML, PDF and other forms. Despite the weaknesses, however, scholars had a central place where online searches could be made and some journal articles, if not all, could be freely retrieved.

Since then, continuous efforts have been made to optimize e-journal databases by augmenting electronic resources and offering better services. Many top academic institutions have participated in the endeavors. For example, the National Central Library has designed and completed its own online e-journal platform and is able to provide access to more journal articles.

Open access movement

There are three Taiwan journals listed in the famous Directory of Open Access Journals: *Chinese Journal of Physics* produced by the Physical Society of the Republic of China, *Journal of Educational Media & Library Sciences* from the Tamkang University Press and *Taiwanese Journal of Mathematics* produced by the Mathematical Society of the Republic of China. Other unlisted journals may also be freely available to users without requiring authentication. The following are examples of open source initiatives in Taiwan that were created to support the online open access movement.

Open Source Software Foundry

The government's Free Software Steering Committee began planning a national FOSS (Free and Open Source Software) project in 2002. Its initiative, Open Source Software Foundry (OSSF), is jointly funded by the Ministry of Economic Affairs, the NSC and the Academia Sinica. The OSSF website is a repository of numerous resources for free software applications. With an easy-to-use platform, members of the FOSS community and academia can use the applications to customize their own prototypes. The OSSF will provide accountability measurement tools to help track, summarize and record activities in project development processes. It will also invite local open source developers to contribute their creativity in software development.

Creative Commons

Creative Commons (CC) Taiwan, a subproject of the OSSF hosted by the Institute of Information Science of the Academia Sinica, was created in 2003. CC Taiwan launched the Creative Commons Licenses in 2004 and has since continued to work with government agencies, civil organizations, collection holders and individual creators. The OSSF has attempted to use the CC licensing model to analyze FOSS licenses in order for new participants to understand them. CC Taiwan has built a web-based platform where both Chinese and English user interfaces are provided so that developers in Taiwan can interact better with one another.

Institutional repositories

Inspired by the open access movement, a few institutional repositories have developed in Taiwan in the past few years. The Taiwan Academic Institutional Repository (TAIR) was developed by the National Taiwan University Library in 2005 and funded by the Ministry of Education. The system was built on the platform of MIT DSpace. The TAIR team has worked on customizing the application to make it Chinese language compatible, enhancing system performance and analyzing usability to improve its functionality. Feng Chia University and the Academia Sinica have also adopted the DSpace software to develop their own institutional repositories. So far these repositories have not achieved a large content size and are still at experimental stages.

Scholarly exchange

During the Japanese colonization, Japanese was the language for education and publishing. Taiwanese scholars were trained with the Japanese scholarly system. After the ROC moved to Taiwan, the American tradition became the model, and more scholarly exchanges were made between Taiwan and the USA. With increased numbers of American-trained scholars, the US influence in the research community was substantial. This was not only noticeable in the fields of science and technology but also in the humanities and social sciences, where research subjects are local in most cases.

Since the 1980s scholarly exchanges between Taiwan and China have dramatically increased due to the change in political climate. There is a strong foundation for the proliferation of scholarly conversations between the two sides of the Strait. Both use the same language and share the same cultural tradition. At the beginning of the new era, the decades-long separation of the two sides aroused great curiosity to explore each other. Both their similarities and their differences became reasons to continue exchange programs. Such a scholarly closeness is strongly supported by the mutual reliance of their economic resources and social undertakings.

Scholarly exchanges between the two sides are now the mainstream. The exchanges have taken varied forms, ranging from carrying out research collaborations and co-authoring articles to attending research events hosted by the other side in almost every academic field. For several consecutive years there have been more scholars from the mainland traveling to Taiwan as visiting scholars than from any other country. It is believed that as soon as political restrictions are lessened and direct flights between the two sides are frequent, more exchanges will be initiated.

Publications from the mainland are largely sold in the market and stocked in libraries of Taiwan, partly because of their cheap prices. The low prices of mainland publications have put pressure on publishers and wholesalers in Taiwan, which have to restructure their publishing and distribution process in order to retain market share. Yet the huge market in mainland China will even out these discrepancies. China uses a simplified form of the Chinese language which was initially unknown to the Taiwanese, but they have now become accustomed to it. On the mainland side, publications in traditional Chinese language, though having been stopped for more than three decades, have also become popular. In the past, imported publications from China focused primarily on the humanities and social sciences such as in archaeology, history and literature, and took the form of series edited by well-known scholars. The future will see more mainland books in sciences, technology and medicine.

Conclusion

Jingfeng Xia

From the previous chapters, readers have seen how cultural, economic and political influences helped shape the tradition of scholarly communication in different regions and countries in East Asia. Throughout history, East Asian countries shared a similar humanities-centered scholarly orientation that was constructed by the widespread influence of Confucianism. Information and knowledge were formed and delivered in analogous ways, resulting in comparable schooling and publishing systems across the area. A pan-East Asian culture, with the intermediary of Chinese characters, was manifested by publications in both their presentation and their contents.

In the past two centuries the introduction of Western culture and technologies into the Far East has changed the terrain of its traditional practices. Each region/country reacted to the exposure to foreign systems in different ways in conjunction with its own situation, so the new development of scholarly communication in East Asia has been characterized by a process of diversification. It is therefore not surprising that while Korean scholars are making great efforts to get through a recent economic turmoil and recovery, Japanese social scientists have become accustomed to a unique system that facilitates the circulation of research data and findings by exchanging institutionally managed *kiyōs* and not relying on a peer-review routine. Similarly, although researchers in Hong Kong are familiar with scholarly practices of the Western style, their Chinese colleagues have to adjust to rapidly increasing commercialization in virtually every aspect of their lives, including scholarly conduct. Both Hong Kong and Taiwanese people have recently been struggling with their ethnic identities as a result of changing relationships with mainland China, and this can inevitably be observed in scholarly communities, where research concentrations are reoriented according to varying geo-political circumstances.

Globalization is another theme in the formation of scholarly communication in East Asia, particularly during the past several decades. Scholars from all regions and countries have progressively worked on standardizing their communication channels in order to promote broader information sharing. The advancement of information technology, particularly the invention and popularity of the internet, has made their globalization efforts easier than ever before. Both Hong Kong and Korea are proud of their networking coverage and usage, while China is catching up quickly with new updates and has done a better job in some areas such as digitization. The aggressive plan of China's digital projects has become a model for Japan and Taiwan.

The process of globalization is also actualized by scholarly exchange activities among these regions and countries as well as between the regions/countries and the rest of the world. Across-country and regional collaborative projects have advanced scientific discoveries and at the same time benefited the development of the scholarly communication structure in each of the regions and countries covered in this book. English is considered to be the standard by which the level of globalization is assessed, and there is an increasing emphasis on publication assessment by citation frequencies among the international community. East Asian scholars and scholarly structures have become an integral part of the world system.

Ever since the introduction of Western scholarship in the eighteenth century, science and technology have been incorporated into the research agenda side by side with, and most recently more centrally to, the long-established humanities preference. This science and technology emphasis was in tandem with the appearance of and improvements in modern education and information preservation and dissemination: libraries have experienced a process of struggle and accomplishment. In each region and country covered in this book, the development of scholarly communication mirrors concurrent economic and political conditions. Fluctuations in economic growth and decline did have a significant impact on academic community-building, while governmental support through funding and policies has been crucial to scholarship. Readers can see from the historical descriptions that every government of these regions and countries has throughout history become actively involved in the making and remaking of regional scholarly communication.

Major developments are highlighted in each chapter, with the support of background explanations and statistics from authoritative resources. Across the entire area, recent developments have benefited from a digital revolution that has redesigned the way information is communicated at the global level. Digital preservations and presentations have changed the definition of publishing and library functions; and information retrieval via online platforms has broadened and accelerated information sharing. All of these regions and countries have planned or actually worked on fostering the initiation and expansion of information and communications technology in the applications of scholarly communication. The achievements have been remarkable.

It is an ongoing challenge for scholars and scholarly communities to balance tradition and innovation, individualization and standardization, and regionalization and internationalization. East Asian regions and countries have been successful in these exertions. Leaving out their struggles in history, recent decades have witnessed how they have survived the strong penetration of commercialization into scholarly purity, as in China and Taiwan, and the economic and financial turmoil of East and South-East Asia in 1997, as in Japan, Korea and Hong Kong. This, of course, does not diminish the fact that they still face challenges of varied types at different levels today. Let us keep optimistic about their future, and appreciate their contributions to the mosaic of the world's scholarly communication.

References

Association of College & Research Libraries (2006) *ACRL Scholarly Communication Toolkit*; available at: *www.ala.org/ala/acrl/acrlissues/ scholarlycomm/scholarlycommunicationtoolkit/faculty/faculty.htm* (accessed: 10 December 2007).

Cao, C. (2004) 'Chinese science and the "Nobel Prize complex"', *Minerva*, 42(2): 151–72.

Calvert, P.J. and Shi, Z. (2001) 'Quality versus quantity: contradictions in LIS journal publishing in China', *Library Management*, 22(4/5): 205–11.

China Internet Network Information Center (2007) 'Statistical survey report on the internet development in China'; available at: *www.cnnic .net.cn/download/2007/20thCNNICreport-en.pdf* (accessed: 11 December 2007).

Chiu, J.Y. and Liu, Y.Y. (2003) 'Problems and solutions in the development of university presses in Taiwan', *Journal of Educational Media and Library Sciences*, 41(1): 77–98.

Cummings, A.M., Witte, M.L., Bowen, W.G., Lazarus, L.O. and Ekman, R.H. (1992) *University Libraries and Scholarly Communication: A Study Prepared for the Andrew W. Mellon Foundation*. Washington, DC: Association of Research Libraries for the Andrew W. Mellon Foundation; available at: *http://etext.virginia.edu/subjects/mellon/ index.html* (accessed: 10 December 2007).

Deutsche Bank Research (2005a) *Human Capital is the Key to Growth: Success Stories and Policies for 2020*; available at: *www.dbresearch.com/ PROD/DBR_INTERNET_EN-PROD/PROD0000000000190080.pdf* (accessed: 11 December 2007).

Deutsche Bank Research (2005b) *Current Issues: Global Growth Centres*; available at: *www.dbresearch.com/PROD/DBR_INTERNET_ EN-PROD/PROD0000000000190080.pdf* (accessed: 11 December 2007).

Government Information Office ROC (ed.) (2006) *The Publication Annual 2006*. Taipei: Government Information Office.

Hanguk Kwahak Kisul Kihoek Pyongkawon (Korea Institute of Science & Technology Evaluation and Planning) (2007) 'Tonggye DB Komsaek (Statistical database)'; available at: *http://kistep.ssdb.co.kr/cgi-bin/sws_999.cgi?ID=DT_AAA0001&IDTYPE=3&A_LANG=1&FPUB=3&SELITEM=* (accessed: 10 December 2007).

Hanguk Kyoyuk Kaebarwon (Korean Educational Development Institute) (2006) *Kyoyuk Tonggye Yonbo (Statistical Yearbook of Education)*. Seoul: Hanguk Kyoyuk Kaebarwon.

Hanguk Taehak Chulpanbu Hyophoe (Association of Korean University Presses) (2007) 'Hyophoe Hoewon (Membership)'; available at: *www.akup.net* (accessed: 11 December 2007).

Hanguk Tosogwan Hyophoe (Korean Library Association) (2006) *Hanguk Tosogwan Yongam*. Seoul Tukpyolsi: Hanguk Tosogwan Hyophoe.

Hong, Song-je (2006) *Hanguk Yonguja ui 2005-yondo SCI Inyong Chisu Punsok Yongu: NCR Korea 1995–2005. Chongchaek Yongu, 2006-songkwa 1*. Seoul: Hanguk Haksul Chinhung Chaedan (Korea Research Foundation).

Huang, C. (1987) 'The structure of Chinese libraries', *Bulletin of the China Society of Library Science*, 4.

Instituto Cultural do Governo da R.A.E. de Macau (2007) 'Macau Central Library'; available at: *http://www3.icm.gov.mo/gate/gb/www.icm.gov.mo/deippub/indexC.asp* (accessed: 10 December 2007).

Kim, Suk-Young (ed.) (2006) *Libraries in Korea: Past, Present, and Future*. Seoul: World Library and Information Congress 2006, Seoul National Organizing Committee.

Korean Educational Development Institute (2006) *Kyoyuk Tonggye Yonbo (Statistical Yearbook of Education)*. Seoul: Hanguk Kyoyuk Kaebarwon.

KOSEF (Korea Science and Engineering Foundation) (2006) 'Budget trends'; available at: *www.kosef.re.kr/english_new/* (accessed: 11 December 2007).

Kyoyuk Inchok Chawon Tonggye Sobisu (Korea National Center for Education & Statistics Information) (2007) 'Web portal'; available at: *cesi.kedi.re.kr/index.jsp* (accessed: 11 December 2007).

Library Association of the Republic of China (Taiwan) and National Central Library (eds) (2007) *Librarianship in Taiwan*, 2nd edn. Taipei: National Central Library.

Library Society of China (2006) 'The vigorous advancement of libraries in China', *IFLA Journal*, 32(2): 113–18.

Lin, S.C. (2005) *Libraries and Librarianship in China*. Westport, CT: Greenwood Press.

Macau SAR Government (2007) 'Government portal'; available at: *www.gov.mo/egi/Portal/index.htm* (accessed: 10 December 2007).

Marx, K. (1867) *Capital (Das Kapital)*, Vol. 1. Hamburg: Kritik der politischen Oekonomie.

Ministry of Education (2007) 'Report on application status of higher educational institutions'; available at: *www.moe.edu.cn* (accessed: 10 December 2007).

Ministry of the Interior (2006) 'Statistics'; available at: *www.moi .gov.tw/stat/main_1.asp?id=2665* (accessed: 11 December 2007).

Mushakoji, S. (1987) 'Nihon ni okeru gakujutsu tosho shuppan tensu no teiryoteki bunseki (Quantitative analysis for scholarly books published in Japan)', *Library and Information Science*, 25: 65–80.

National Bureau of Statistics of China (2007) *China Statistical Yearbook*. Beijing: China Statistics Press.

National Science Council of Taiwan (2003) *Macro Level Bibilometric Analysis of Taiwanese Science*. Taipei: Science and Technology Information Center.

National Science Indicators (2005) CD-ROM. Philadelphia, PA: Thomson Scientific.

OECD (2003a) *Programme for International Student Assessment (PISA) 2003 Country Profiles*: available at: *www.pisa.oecd.org/document/ 50/0,3343,en_32252351_32236173_37627442_1_1_1_1,00.html* (accessed: 11 December 2007).

OECD (2003b) *OECD Science, Techonology and Industry Scoreboard*. Paris: Organization for Economic Cooperation and Development.

OECD (2006) *OECD Factbook 2006: Economic, Environmental and Social Statistics*. Paris: Organization for Economic Cooperation and Development.

OECD (2007a) *R&D Expenditure by Source of Financing, 2005, OECD Science, Technology and Industry Scoreboard*; available at: *http://dx.doi.org/10.1787/116676883373* (accessed: 10 December 2007).

OECD (2007b) 'Main science and technology indicators'; available at: *http://stats.oecd.org/wbos/Default.aspx?usercontext=sourceoecd* (accessed: 15 December 2007).

Peking University Library (2007) 'Introduction to Peking University Library'; available at: *www.lib.pku.edu.cn/portal/portal/media-type/ html/group/pkuguest/page/benguanjianjie.psml* (accessed: 10 December 2007).

Publishers Association of China (1980) *China Publishing Yearbook.* Beijing: Commercial Press.

Publishers Association of China (1981) *China Publishing Yearbook.* Beijing: Commercial Press.

Publishers Association of China (1983) *China Publishing Yearbook.* Beijing: Commercial Press.

Publishers Association of China (1984) *China Publishing Yearbook.* Beijing: Commercial Press.

Publishers Association of China (1994) *China Publishing Yearbook.* Beijing: Publishers Association of China Press.

Publishers Association of China (2000) *China Publishing Yearbook.* Beijing: Publishers Association of China Press.

Science Citation Index (2005) CD-ROM. Philadelphia, PA: Institute for Scientific Information.

Taehak Chulpan Munhwa Hyophoe (2006) *Hanguk Chulpan Yongam (Korean Publication Yearbook)*, Vol. 1. Seoul: Hanguk Chulpan Munhwa Hyophoe (Korean Publishers Association).

Thomson Scientific (2004) *The Year 2004: Top 20 Country Rankings in All Fields*; available at: *http://in-cites.com/countries/2004allfields.html* (accessed: 15 December 2007).

Thomson Scientific (2005) *Science in South Korea, 1999–2003*; available at: *http://in-cites.com/research/2005/february_7_2005-1.html* (accessed: 15 December 2007).

University Grants Committee (1999) 'Research assessment exercise 1999 – local universities achieve remarkable research results'; available at: *www.ugc.edu.hk/eng/ugc/publication/prog/rae/rae.htm* (accessed: 10 December 2007).

University Grants Committee (2006) 'Excellent results from the research assessment exercise 2006'; available at: *www.ugc.edu.hk/eng/ugc/publication/prog/rae/rae.htm* (accessed: 10 December 2007).

Wu, Y., Pan, Y., Zhang, Y., Ma, Z., Pang, J., Guo, H., Xu, B. and Yang, Z. (2004) 'China scientific and technical papers and citations (CSTPC): history, impact and outlook', *Scientometrics*, 60(3): 385–97.

Xia, J. (2006) 'Scholarly communication in East and Southeast Asia: traditions and challenges', *IFLA Journal*, 32(2): 104–12.

Yi, Chae-min (2005) 'Opun Aksesu rul Wihan Haksul Nonmun ui Chojakkwon Kwisok Hyonhwang kwa Kaeson Pangan (Problems with copyright ownership of scholarly journal articles in Korea)', master's thesis, Department of Library & Information Science, Graduate School, Daegu University.

Yun, Chong-gwang (2000) *Hanguk Chulpan Sanop Siltae Chosa* (*Survey on the Current State of the Korean Publishing Industry*). Seoul: Hanguk Chulpan Yonguso.

Yun, Hui-yun (2005) 'Kukka Kwahak Kisul Chongbo Chawon Kaebal Mohyong Yongu (A study on the development model of STM information resources in Korea)', *Yongu Pogoso*, K-05-ID-01-01R-5. Seoul: Hanguk Kwahak Kisul Chongbo Yonguwon (Korea Institute of Science and Technology Information).

Yun, Hui-yun (2007) 'OECD Kukka Kyongjaengnyok mit Yolngu Kyongjaengnyok ui Sangwan Punsok (Correlation analysis between competitiveness and national research competitiveness in OECD countries)', *Hanguk Munhon Chongbo Hakhoe chi*, 41(1).

Zhang, W. (2003) 'Classification for Chinese libraries (CCL): histories, accomplishments, problems and its comparisons', *Journal of Educational Media & Library Sciences,* 41(1): 1–22.

Zheng, L. (2004) 'Print and electronic resources for Chinese studies: current trends', paper presented at Chinese American Librarians Association Midwest Chapter Annual Program, University of Illinois, Urbana-Champaign, 1 May.

Index

Printed and bound by CPI Group (UK) Ltd, Croydon, CR0 4YY

08/05/2025

01864968-0003